Sweden's
    "Right to be
Human"

HILDA SCOTT

Sweden's *"Right to be* *Human"* SEX-ROLE EQUALITY:
THE GOAL AND THE REALITY

R Routledge
Taylor & Francis Group

LONDON AND NEW YORK

First published 1982 by M.E. Sharpe

Reissued 2018 by Routledge
2 Park Square, Milton Park, Abingdon, Oxon OX14 4RN
711 Third Avenue, New York, NY 10017, USA

Routledge is an imprint of the Taylor & Francis Group, an informa business

A Library of Congress record exists under LC control number: 81005239

ISBN 13: 978-1-138-03789-2 (hbk)
ISBN 13: 978-1-138-03793-9 (pbk)
ISBN 13: 978-1-315-17762-5 (ebk)

Contents

Introduction

The motion picture *Kramer vs. Kramer*, in which a young father sets out to prove that he has all the qualities of a good mother, and in the process relinquishes the high-pressure career that is just within his grasp, won five Oscars in 1980. It is hard to remember today that only ten years ago a suggestion that the respective parts played by men and women in society and personal life are (with the exception of childbearing) assigned somewhat arbitrarily by society and not by nature, still had some of the impact that Darwin's theory of the origin of species had had a century before. The possibility that the traits of personality and behavior designated as "feminine" and "masculine" were more the product of conditioning and cultural tradition than of genes or hormones was a subject to be introduced in mixed company at one's own risk.

The need for women in the labor force in the boom years of the 1960s and the widespread introduction of the birth-control pill were the chief determinants of a "sexual revolution" in the Western world whose theoretical premises were as yet undefined. Social scientists were studying women in the family, "role expectations," "role confusion," and "role conflicts," women's educational choices, and the socialization of children, but very few were *questioning* the roles they described. Male roles were largely ignored.[1] A breakthrough in sex-role research was the publication in 1966 by Eleanor Maccoby at Stanford University of a collection of studies by scholars in several fields, examining the level of knowledge concerning the relative roles of biological determinants and social demands in the development of sex differences. The authors found no firm evidence of important behavioral characteristics that inherently belonged to one sex or the other.[2]

In the United States, still in the grip of the suburban ideal, sociologist Alice Rossi was in 1964 a lone voice arguing that since by far the majority of the "differences" between the sexes were socially determined, a new definition of sex equality was called for. She advanced "a socially androgynous conception of the roles of men and women":

> Each sex will cultivate some of the characteristics usually associated with the other in traditional sex-role definitions. This means that tenderness and expressiveness should be cultivated in boys and socially approved in men . . . that achievement need, workmanship and constructive aggression should be cultivated in girls and approved in women . . . . This definition of sex equality stresses the enlargement of the common ground on which men and women base their lives together by changing the social definitions of approved characteristics and behavior for both sexes.[3]

Rossi deplored that there was "practically no feminist spark left among American women." She regretted what she saw as the excessive and unhealthy involvement of American women in homemaking and childrearing, their absorption with marriage, and she outlined the first institutional steps that could bring closer a more equal division of social roles between men and women: day care for preschool children, a change in the American pattern of suburban living, and changes in the school curriculum. While her view of the future did not then include an equal division of tasks in the home, she thought both men and women would come to agree "that unless a man can make room in his life for parenthood, he should not become a father."[4]

When the "feminist spark" was lit—in fact, in the very year in which Rossi wrote—women's energies at first were directed primarily at recognizing and describing their oppression. The 1963 report of the President's Commission on the Status of Women, while recommending the removal of barriers to women's full participation in the life of society, assumed that women would continue to bear the main responsibility for children and the home. The inclusion of women under Title VII of the Civil Rights Act in 1964 occurred almost by accident, and was seen by most congressmen as a joke.[5] As late as 1972, "sex roles" rated only five entries in the index of U.S. literature in the social sciences; by 1975 this number had expanded to 56.

It was in the latter year that the first major statement forwarding a practical program for a more equal division of roles ap-

peared in the United States in the form of a report by the Twentieth Century Fund Task Force on Women and Employment, *Exploitation from 9 to 5*.[6] Its recommendations called for
  —affirmative action plans by employers;
  —enforcement of equal opportunity legislation;
  —more militancy by trade unions;
  —the elimination of sex-role stereotypes in education;
  —universally available high-quality day care;
  —the use of government social-security, income-tax, welfare, and training programs to equalize the position of women and men.

By the time this document appeared, the concept of sex-role equality had already acquired a certain international respectability through its incorporation in a United Nations document. This was the report of the World Conference of the International Women's Year, held in Mexico City from June 19 to July 5, 1975. Point 16 of the Plan of Action reads:

> The achievement of equality between men and women implies that they should have equal rights, opportunities and responsibilities to enable them to develop their talents and capabilities for their own personal fulfillment and the benefit of society. To that end, a reassessment of the functions and roles traditionally allotted to each sex within the family and the community at large is essential. The necessity of a change in the traditional role of men as well as women must be recognized.[7]

If so diverse a group as the delegates to the IWY conference in Mexico City could agree to such a statement of principles (in preference to the more conservative amendments offered by the Soviet Union and Japan, which called for conditions to enable women to combine their duties in the home with activities outside it), this was at least in part because of the arguments and concrete experience of Scandinavian delegates, who were able to point to already functioning government programs and legislation aimed at changing the daily lives of both women and men. It is this legislation, these programs, and this experience, as they were shaped in Sweden specifically, that I will examine in the following chapters.

I made my first visit to Sweden in 1968. At that time I was in the process of gathering material for a book on the situation of women in Eastern European countries—where, it was officially claimed, the abolition of private property had already emancipated women and full equality with men would inevitably follow.[8] In real life, however, a debate was in full swing concerning the intense conflicts women were experiencing in combining their "two roles" as wage-earners and homemakers. The conviction was so deeply ingrained there that women's problems would be solved, as in Engels's formula, when housekeeping was transformed into a public industry and the care of children became a public matter,[9] that no one thought to ask the question, Are these really just "women's problems"? Since it was obvious that society was in no way prepared to fulfill Engels's conditions, I shared the general pessimism concerning the real possibilities of minimizing one of women's roles to the point where it would no longer be a handicap that disqualified her for equality from the very start.

It was then that I made the acquaintance in Sweden of the simple premise that one cannot change women's position without changing men's, and the proposition that if roles are socially rather than biologically determined, there is no reason why they cannot be shared equally by women and men. Under such circumstances one need not wait for the millenium when an anonymous "society" would take over the children and the "nonproductive" household chores and thus free women for "productive" work. One could make a beginning, at least, by designing policies that would help to equalize the distribution of burdens and benefits between women and men, while still working for the public supports that would lighten the drudgery in individual households.

Since that time I have paid two longer visits to Sweden to follow the progress of its sex-role equality program. On the first occasion, in 1975, I found that some important legislative steps had already been taken and a number of pilot projects were under way. Although it was realized that changing the roles of men and women was a long and complicated process, there was considerable optimism concerning the effect these first steps would have. Four years later, at the end of 1979, I found that in spite of many innovative and carefully considered government measures, which in their sum total go well beyond what has been achieved in other countries, there was a prevailing air of dissatisfaction. Great efforts seemed to have produced small results.

Though conscious of my limitations as an outsider, I have set down what I learned because it seems to me that Sweden's experience is of unusual importance for all women and men who are actively concerned with how to achieve greater equality between the sexes, and that this is so in spite of the fact that no other country has exactly the same conditions or is likely to duplicate the experiment in just this form. It illustrates how much can be accomplished in a welfare state that is prepared to invest in equality; at the same time it exposes the areas where women and men have conflicting interests that cannot be reached by such reforms. In doing so it confirms, in my opinion, what some people in the women's movement and outside it have already come to believe: that equality is not just a matter of public spending or even of public ownership, important as these may be, but of a fundamentally different concept of society that will take both "male" and "female" needs and values into account. Through the Swedish experience we can even perceive some of the outlines of such a society.

In this book my main purpose has been to follow the genesis, the effects, and the side effects of the measures to achieve sex-role equality that have been taken, and to identify the obstacles that have prevented them from being fully effective. I have also tried to record the feedback of these events on the sex-role equality drive and on the attitudes of women particularly. In conclusion I have ventured to predict in a very general way the direction that work for equality will take in the future.

In the course of my three visits to Sweden I interviewed well over a hundred people—some in key positions at a national or local level, some engaged in a very practical and specific way in working for sex-role equality, and some just "average" women and men who were trying to fit their personal lives into the pattern of new possibilities and old stereotypes. Because so many Swedes speak English well, I was able to work without an interpreter on all but a few occasions. I also benefited from the considerable amount of written material on sex-role equality by Swedish agencies and individual authors that is available in English.

A note about terminology: I am aware that there is dissatisfaction among social scientists with the term "sex roles." Some find "role" inaccurate to describe learned behavior differentiated by biological sex. Others argue that the use of "sex roles" to refer to all the characteristics and attitudes attributed to women and men helps to perpetuate misconceptions regarding an inevitable relationship between biological and social influences. They recommend "gender roles" for behavior determined by psychological and socio-cultural factors and would reserve "sex" for the biological and physiological only.[10] In this book I have used "sex roles" and "sex-role equality" throughout, first of all because it is used consistently in the Swedish and other literature referred to. To introduce competing terminology would create confusion rather than clarity. Moreover, at this stage of the argument I believe that these are still the terms most easily understood by most people.

I take this opportunity to thank all those in Sweden who so generously gave me their time and shared their frank opinions with me. I owe a particular debt of gratitude to Annika Baude, who first introduced me to Sweden and ever since has offered me encouragement, practical help, and a continuing dialogue. I should like to express my sincere appreciation to The Swedish Institute in Stockholm, and particularly to Kerstin Pehrsson and Catharina Mannheimer who arranged my study trips with so much care. Finally, thanks are due to my husband, Herbert Lass, for editorial suggestions on the entire manuscript, and to Professor Joan M. McCrae of the Economics Department of the University of Texas, Arlington, for her pertinent comments on several chapters. Any errors of fact or interpretation are, of course, my own.

Hilda Scott

Vienna,
July 1980

Notes

1. See Jean Lipman-Blumen and Ann R. Tickamyer, "Sex Roles in Transition: A Ten-Year Perspective," *Annual Review of Sociology* 1 (1975): 297-337; Reesa M. Vaughter, "Psychology: Review Essay," *Signs* 2, no. 1 (1976): 120-46.

2. E. E. Maccoby, ed., *The Development of Sex Differences* (Stanford, Ca.: Stanford University Press, 1966).

3. Alice S. Rossi,"Equality Between the Sexes: An Immodest Proposal," *Daedalus*, Spring 1964, p. 608.

4. Ibid., p. 649.

5. For accounts of the passage of Title VII see Betty Friedan, *It Changed My Life: Writings on The Women's Movement* (New York: Random House,

1976), p. 78, and Donald Allen Robinson, "Two Movements in Pursuit of Equal Employment Opportunity," *Signs* 4, no. 3 (1979): 413.

6. *Exploitation from 9 to 5: Report of the Twentieth Century Task Force on Women and Employment* (New York: Lexington Books, 1975).

7. "Report of the World Conference of the International Women's Year," United Nations Economic and Social Council, E/5725, July 11, 1975, p. 9.

8. Hilda Scott, *Does Socialism Liberate Women?: Experiences from Eastern Europe* (Boston: Beacon Press, 1974); published in Great Britain as *Women and Socialism* (London: Allison & Busby, 1976).

9. Frederick Engels, *The Origin of the Family, Private Property and the State* (Moscow: Foreign Languages Publishing House, 1948) p. 108.

10. For some recent arguments regarding the use of "sex roles" and "gender roles," see Helen Z. Lopata and Barrie Thorne, "On the Term 'Sex Roles,'" *Signs*, 3, no. 3 (1978): 718-21, and J. Martin Graham & Cannie Stark-Adamec, "Sex and Gender: The Need for Redefinition," *Resources for Feminist Research*, 9, no. 2 (1980): 7. A plea in defense of "sex roles" is entered by Alice Henry in "Comment on 'On the Term *Sex Roles*,'" *Signs*, 4, no. 4 (1979): 812-13.

Sweden's
"Right to be
Human"

CHAPTER 1

Equality is the Goal

In 1968 Sweden became the first country in the world to frame a government policy of achieving equality between the sexes by changing the role of men as well as that of women. In a statement to the United Nations that year the Swedish government had declared that it was not enough to guarantee women their rights. All legislation and all social policy must support a shift from man-the-breadwinner and woman-the-homemaker to a society of independent individuals and of partnerships in which all tasks were shared:

> The aim of a *long-term* "programme for women" must be that every individual, irrespective of sex, shall have the same *practical* opportunities, not only for education and employment, but also in principle the same responsibility for his or her own maintenance as well as shared responsibility for the upbringing of children and the upkeep of the home . . . . The government is well aware that this view appears revolutionary and unrealistic in the eyes of the representatives of many other countries. A growing opinion in Sweden has, however, rallied to its support.[1]

In Sweden as in other Scandinavian countries, the statement continued, a debate had already been under way for six or seven years concerning the division of roles between women and men in the home and in society, and had resulted in a departure from "the traditional habit of regarding these problems as 'women's questions.' "

It follows that well before the modern women's movement gained momentum in North America and Europe, the drive for women's "emancipation" had been rechristened the "sex-role debate" in Scandinavia and expanded to include "men's emancipation" as well. That such a debate should have had the most emphatic response in Sweden was only logical. It was in Sweden, of all the

3

Western countries, that employment of women rose most sharply between 1950 and 1960, and the consequences could hardly escape analysis in a society so sensitized to issues of social responsibility. Whereas in most countries it was still accepted as the nature of things that women were in demand for and drawn into the low-paid jobs, and that they did the housework and took care of the children as well, at least some Swedes were quick to see that something was wrong and to say so.

Credit for being the first in Sweden to frame the problem as one of men's need for emancipation as well as women's is usually given jointly to a prominent woman journalist, Barbro Alving, and to Karin Westman-Berg, now professor of literature at the University of Uppsala and responsible for the first courses in Sweden that could be described as "women's studies." At a meeting in 1957 of the Fredrika Bremer Association, the country's oldest women's organization (dating from 1884), Westman-Berg asked:

> Should we abet men in their efforts to suppress affection and emancipate themselves from emotional considerations? They have a vast backlog to make up for after all the thousands of years for which their development potential has been smothered. Are we going to accept partial responsibility for half of mankind being kept at an infantile stage of development, especially in view of the dangerous toys they like playing with?[2]

Meanwhile, in practice Swedish housewives were acclimatizing themselves to what was then the new life-style for women, the one foreseen by Alva Myrdal—one of Sweden's foremost social scientists and public figures—in the book she co-authored with Viola Klein in 1956, *Women's Two Roles*. The authors, while favoring the view that mothers should stay home with their children in the earliest years if possible, advocated their return to gainful occupation once the children were older, and called for the provision of services to lighten housework. Their further recommendations are prophetic in retrospect, although at the time they seemed to go unnoticed. Klein and Myrdal concluded that "making husbands and fathers full partners in the affairs of their families seems highly desirable. The employment of women past childbearing age should make possible the shortening of the working day," and a six-hour workday for both men and women "would make a complete renaissance of home life possible."[3] They did not raise the question as to whether men would take willingly to this pattern.

It is usual to pinpoint the real beginning of the sex-role debate in Sweden from the publication in 1961 of an essay called "The Conditional Emancipation of Women" by Eva Moberg, a popular journalist and editor of the Fredrika Bremer Association's bimonthly, *Herta*. She argued, as a prospective mother, that there was nothing about the act of childbirth that required her to be the one who would go on diapering, feeding, and caring for the child until it became an adult. She rejected the idea that woman had an inherent "main function"—childcare and homemaking—and that anything else she did was secondary.

"We ought to stop harping on the concept of 'women's two roles,' " she wrote. "Both men and women have *one* principal role, that of being people." Moberg reacted to her many and sometimes vituperous attackers by carrying the argument even further. She predicted that the day would come when women would no longer have the exclusive "right to choose" between home and a career, that both men and women would have the same options and the same obligations toward society.[4]

Moberg was not fighting alone. She was the advance guard for a Swedish-Norwegian group of sociologists, economists, and psychologists who in 1962 published the results of their four years of investigations in a book called *Women's Life and Work*. (This appeared in an abridged and updated version as *The Changing Roles of Men and Women* in Great Britain in 1967 and in the United States in 1971.) It provided a documented, multidisciplinary approach to what were then the most combustible issues— the effect of women's work on family life, the effect on the child of the mother's absence from the home and of parental role division, and the impact of traditional ideas of sex differences on women's job opportunities. In the process it disposed of two conventional arguments, the conservative (women's place is in the home) and the liberal (something should be done to diminish the conflict of women's two roles). It showed how the culturally conditioned expectations imposed on an individual freeze her or him into a mold and impoverish both sexes and society as well. It concluded that women and men have one role, and where there are children this includes childcare.

The researchers had their own backup group of opinion makers from the media and from various organizations who had been meeting informally to discuss sociopolitical issues for some time. They saw to it that the book was widely reviewed and discussed. It provided a bulwark of facts and figures against the waves of emotion that accompanied the general revival of discussion of women's issues in the 1960s. Even the political parties began to realize that this was an issue they could not sidestep. Here the Social Democratic women's organization played a crucial role in bringing home to the ruling Social Democratic Party the realization that it must incorporate the goals of sex-role equality in its program.

"We forced the Party to form a study group in 1960," recalls Lisa Mattson, who for many years has been the president of the National Federation of Social Democratic Women and a member of Parliament. This study group on "women's questions" had as its honorary chairman the then Prime Minister, Tage Erlander. Its acting chairperson was a diplomat, Inga Thorsson, and among its other women members was Minister for Social Affairs Ulla Lindström. Maj-Britt Sandlund—who was later to author Sweden's report to the United Nations on the status of women, quoted at the beginning of this chapter—was secretary of the study group. All the basic aims of sex-role equality that were later to be implemented in legislation and in social, educational, and labor-market policy were suggested by this study group in "The Erlander Report," which was adopted by the party in 1964.

It was not until 1969, however, that its proposals were approved as part of the party program by the Social Democrat's party congress, when they appeared embedded in the policy declaration drawn up by a working group on equality questions chaired by Alva Myrdal. This document said in so many words that government powers over industry were to be used to eliminate sex discrimination, that labor-market and educational policies must counteract sex-determined choices of occupation, and that expanded services, especially day care and public transport, were essential requirements for an effective equality policy. "In the society of the future," it added, "when current practical barriers to equality have been gradually eliminated, the point of departure must be that every adult is responsible for his/her own support. Benefits previously inherent in married status should be eliminated or transferred to children. . . . Adults should be treated in the same manner by society whether they live alone or in some form of common living arrangement." [5]

Insofar as this statement of aims gained broad acceptance in the ranks of the Social Democratic Party and the blue-collar trade unions that make up the most important section of its membership and voters, it was because the political technique that had been used in the 1930s, when Sweden became famous for its "middle way" between socialism and capitalism, had proved its effectiveness once more. Just as Sweden's early social measures were accepted because they were presented as the solution to a "population crisis" which then concerned everyone deeply, so the sex-role equality program was assimilated because it was part of an "equality program" that had something for everybody. In 1968 an "equality" platform had carried the Social Democrats to their greatest postwar victory. The 1969 report of the Working Group on Equality elaborated the principles underlying the party's view of equality and recommended concrete measures for implementing campaign promises. The program's overall purpose was to "restore the balance" for all less-privileged groups—the young, the old, the handicapped, the unemployed, the low-income groups, and the rural dwellers—as well as women. Thus some of the more fiercely debated measures relating to the status of women (or the status of men) were packaged so that the inclusion of women was only implicit. Among the recommendations adopted by the party congress in 1969 were:

—the reduction of wage differentials between low and high earners;

—reassessment of the relative values of occupations requiring mental and physical abilities;

—a tax policy based on individual earnings, without regard to "form of cohabitation";

—labor-market measures to create jobs and provide training especially designed for individual target groups;

—day care as a benefit to children as well as parents;

—incorporation of sex-role questions in the school curriculum at all stages of the educational process, and the elimination from textbooks of traditional assumptions about male and female roles;

—the planning of housing areas, both old and new, to include services and facilities to meet the diverse needs of the residents—working parents, pensioners, young people, and children;

—long-range changes in the social insurance system, to be based on the individual without regard to marital status;

—freer regulations governing marriage, and more protection for other forms of cohabitation.

This document was to provide the guidelines for the Social Democratic equality policy on the local and national level. Meanwhile, legislation was already being prepared on a number of major issues. The first steps toward the realization of greater equality between the sexes were taken in the early seventies.

The phasing out of streaming, or tracking, in the comprehensive school curriculum, which tended to divide boys and girls according to sex-determined interests, began in 1968. A new elementary-school curriculum introduced in 1970–71 made sewing, metal- and woodworking, domestic science, and infant care compulsory for both sexes.

The tax reform of 1971 provided for individual tax returns without regard for the earnings of the partner, eliminating the compulsory joint return for married couples and thus the tax disadvantage that occurred when a wife undertook gainful employment. A small tax credit for dependent wives has been preserved temporarily, but as it has not been adjusted to meet inflation it has steadily lost value. A future is foreseen in which a man will no longer realize a tax advantage when his wife remains at home to care for his personal needs.

An Advisory Council on Equality between Men and Women, appointed by the government, began work in 1973 with the task of proposing measures to advance the right of women to work on the same basis as men.

The first-stage reform of the Family Law, effective in 1974, simplified divorce proceedings, permitting immediate divorce if both partners agreed and there were no minor children. In cases of divorce or separation, the law strengthened the right of the father to apply for custody of any children, whether born in or out of wedlock.

"Parental benefits," introduced in 1974, replaced all "maternity benefits." Leave after the birth of a child, amounting at that time to six months, could be divided by the parents as they saw fit, with insurance compensating for 90 percent of pay. Both parents also became eligible for benefits paid during absence from work to care for a sick child.

The characteristics that made it possible for Swedish society to move with relative rapidity from loyal adherence to the idea that woman's first commitment is to her family and man's to his job to acceptance, or at least tolerance, of the idea of a redivision of social roles and even gender characteristics, must be sought in the same complex of circumstances that made Sweden a welfare pioneer. The chief elements of this complex are usually given as its wealth of natural resources and geographical position, its long-standing neutrality, and the absence in its history of autocratic feudal and church authority. Sweden is the fourth largest country in Europe in land area, twice the size of England, with—until recently—an unusually homogeneous population. It is rich in forests, water, and mineral resources. Geographically on the periphery and removed from the world's trouble spots, it long ago relinquished imperialist ambitions (having fought its last war in 1814). Because of the sparsity of its population and the absence of early laws to prevent the parceling out of land among heirs, Sweden lacked the concentrated settlements necessary for an agriculture based on serfdom. The soil, moreover, was poor, and this too probably discouraged large-scale cultivation dependent on subject labor. Consequently the Swedes, unlike the neighboring Danes, were hardly exposed to the rigidities of the feudal system. They remained for the most part outside European power struggles, a country of poor peasant freeholders.[6] Protestantism took hold early in Sweden, and Lutheranism became the official religion in 1593.

For all these reasons, change has proceeded gradually since the Middle Ages, almost without dramatic conflict—in striking contrast to most of the rest of Europe. The existence of a large class of small- and medium-size farmers who from early times participated in both central government and local affairs, helped to establish a tradition of popular participation. As Alva Myrdal has put it, "If democracy could not develop successfully in Scandinavia, given by historical chance quite exceptionally advantageous conditions, it will probably not work anywhere else."[7]

Sweden entered the Industrial Revolution very late, after the middle of the nineteenth century. In 1870 three-quarters of the working population was engaged in farming, forestry, and fishing, with only 9 percent in manufacture or crafts. At this time nearly 45 percent of the British labor force was already working in industry. Swedish industrialization centered around the mining and metal industries, significant for the later development of a techno-

logical tradition, and in wood and paper, for which there was a demand abroad. Much of the new work force came not from the
ranks of artisans but from the rural landless, and was diffused in
backwoods areas near raw-material resources rather than forming a
compact urban proletariat.

The Swedish Social Democratic Party also came late on the
scene, and had a correspondingly different history from its European counterparts in the international socialist movement. While
the first, largest, and most powerful of the socialist parties formed
under the influence of Marxist ideas was the German, established
in 1869, followed by the Dutch party in 1870 and the Danish in
1871, Sweden's was not founded until 1889. Its formative years
fall into the period when Social Democracy was moving away
from revolutionary theory and toward dominance by trade unionism and a practical reformist policy. Although nationalization of
the means of production might still have been the ultimate goal,
day-to-day struggle and parliamentary maneuvering were the strategy. This pragmatic model was especially attractive to Sweden. Although the Social Democratic Party was created as the political
expression of the growing trade-union movement, the city-based
working class was small, class lines were still blurred, and the party
had to appeal to a much broader base, including small farmers,
shopkeepers, and artisans.

Walter Korpi of the Swedish Institute for Social Research, in
his history of Swedish trade unionism centered around the politics
of the powerful Metalworkers' Union, offers what seems a key explanation for Sweden's ability to absorb advanced social policy
without having had a revolutionary tradition. Because of late industrialization and the circumstances that enabled the Social Democratic Party to represent the interests of diverse sections of the less
privileged, once industrialization really got under way the new
large generation of workers inherited a trade-union movement that
had been defined from the start as socialist and had a party of its
own that was already "a major contender for political power."[8]
The situation was therefore quite different from that in Great Britain, for example, where trade unions were split by widely differing
political and religious influences for half a century before the
Labour Party, which claimed to speak for them, finally rose to
prominence after World War I. From the beginning, the Swedish
industrial working class has been highly organized and politically

united around a social program whose goals acquired increasing respectability as the party maintained itself in power for decade after decade (from 1932 to 1976). So generally accepted is the idea of state intervention that only the Conservatives (typically, in Sweden, known as the Moderate Party), with a maximum 20 percent of the vote (1979), speak on behalf of a "socially guided market economy." The Center Party (18 percent in 1979) aims at "a democratic welfare society" with protection of the environment the major goal. The Liberals (11 percent) distinguish themselves from the Social Democrats by rejecting socialism as an ultimate solution, but at the same time they want state measures to protect the weak and have played the role of gadfly on many social-welfare questions. The Communists (5 percent) want more radical social legislation, and the sooner the better. Thus, although the parties may disagree fiercely on specific issues, none would undertake to dismantle the Welfare State.

Sweden did not invent modern social policy. Credit for the first legislation to ameliorate the effects of industrialization through a national system of social insurance goes to Chancellor Otto von Bismarck, who in the 1880s established a scheme of compulsory sickness, accident, and old-age pension insurance in the Germany of Kaiser Wilhelm I. Britain was another pioneer, introducing accident insurance for workers in 1897, and, in the crisis years before the First World War, under pressure from the opposition Labour Party, an old-age pension scheme and the Health and Unemployment Insurance Acts. The subject of worker insurance had been raised in the Scandinavian countries even before Bismarck undertook to "vaccinate Germany against Marxism," and they were stimulated by these examples to follow suit. Sweden's first social insurance, in 1901, introduced limited compensation in cases of occupational accidents, and for a long time, except for a voluntary scheme of state-subsidized sickness insurance, this was the only protection provided against loss of earnings. Sweden's preeminence in welfare-state building since the 1930s is due to the way it has combined social insurance and family policy in a coordinated scheme directed at prevention and protection as well as relief and intended, moreover, to bring about greater equality. Although already the strongest party in the country in the 1920s, the Swedish Social Democratic Party did not come to power until 1932, and then in alliance with the Agrarian Party (now the Center Party). Together they represented the two groups most gravely threatened by the worldwide economic depression that had begun in 1929. This coalition, elected on an anti-unemployment platform, laid the foundation for the first comprehensive state-supported welfare program combined with the first attempt to put Keynesian pump-priming into practice. Public works financed by borrowing were used to create jobs; price supports were offered to farmers; and a "population policy" was adopted which grew into a broad program of family support. Expanding as it did into the fields of health, education, and housing, this policy established the principle once and for all in Sweden that a legitimate purpose of government was not only to save its poorest citizens from sinking further, but to narrow the economic and social gaps between various groups of the population.

Attempts to control population "surpluses" and "shortages" are one of the recurring themes of social history. The poverty that gripped preindustrial Sweden in the nineteenth century, caused by a rise in the landless unemployed and coinciding with an increase in the rate of population growth (due primarily to the decline in mortality rates), had in part been solved by emigration. One million out of a population of less than six million left Sweden between 1860 and 1914, most of them for the United States. When the mortality curve began to level out, however, and the effects of emigration, late marriage, and industrialization began to be felt, alarm over a "population surplus" turned into concern at the prospect of a steadily shrinking Swedish nation—a prospect that alarmed almost everyone. The net fertility rate had fallen below 1.0 by 1927, and by 1934 had reached 0.70; in other words, the population was no longer reproducing itself. By the latter year, unemployment seemed well on the way to solution, and public interest focused on the possibility of turning the ebbing population tide.

It was at this point that the revolution in attitude occurred that put Sweden in the lead as far as experiments in peaceful social change are concerned and explains why in the 1960s Sweden was able to get a consensus for its sex-role equality program. In pursuit of a goal that seemed to them of utmost importance. Swedes became used to the idea that social policies, to be effective, cannot be applied individually, like bandaids or the legendary finger in the dike, but must be part of a consistent program. While France, the

only contender in the field of pronatal policy at that time, limited
itself to offering cash bonuses to large families, Sweden accepted
the premise that "a population policy can be nothing less than a
social policy at large." This was the thesis put forward by Alva and
Gunnar Myrdal in 1934 in their book *Crisis and Population* (published in English for the first time in 1941 in an expanded version
by Alva Myrdal, under the title *Nation and Family*). Of this book
the Swedish sociologist Rita Liljeström writes:

> The authors combined two political perspectives which had not been
> linked together before. . . . Population policy suddenly became a lever
> for socialists for far reaching socio-political reforms in collaboration
> with the conservatives, who were prepared to bank on the preservation
> of the Swedish national stock.[9]

The discussions around this book and the social reforms it suggested established a pattern that was used again later in the sex-
role debate sparked by Moberg's "The Conditional Emancipation
of Women" and by the study *Women's Life and Work* in the
1960s. As Myrdal herself describes it, for a year the country was
blanketed with information on the population question. Radio
carried a series of lectures and debates; study groups were formed
all over the country with material supplied by the broadcasting
company and the Workers' Education Association. Books and pam-
phlets multiplied. Every newspaper and magazine carried articles,
jokes, and letters to the editor. Efforts to attack the discussion as
"indecent" only helped to keep the subject alive. Myrdal writes:

> It cannot be denied that it is more difficult to face squarely problems
> of population which may touch clandestine sexual problems in people's
> own lives than it is to face other social questions. The discussion was
> far from harmonious and peaceful, but a general debate throughout the
> nation was obtained not only on birth control but also on the double
> standard of sexual morality, the disharmony between conventional
> standards and actual behavior, and the differences in attitudes toward
> sexual problems between young and old. The lancing of the boil of pub-
> lic dishonesty was painful but it was lanced.[10]

By the time the discussion ended, the public had accepted the
Myrdals' thesis and its corollary, that "society will shoulder responsibility for the security of the preproductive age group—the

children—as well as for the postproductive one, the aged," as the main framework for a positive family policy.[11]

The policies adopted were not directed at "poor families." All children were deemed to be equally entitled to support. The goal was to reduce the cost of childrearing for the individual family, and at the same time to ensure a degree of leveling among children by making certain benefits in kind available to them automatically. The Population Commission appointed by the government to bring in proposals for legislation issued some seventeen reports between 1935 and 1938, and most of its recommendations were accepted and incorporated into law. Among the reforms were provisions for

—free delivery care and a maternity bonus for all women, and state maternity clinics;

—public housing schemes for families with three or more children, and rent reductions according to the size of family;

—state loans to married couples, and sizable tax exemptions for families with children;

—subsidies for school meals, children's clothing, and play schools for children.

What was way-breaking about the accomplishments of the Population Commission and its committees was not only the comprehensive nature of the support program for children—provided for the first time in a country with a market economy—but the fact that it incorporated legislation that could not be regarded as a direct stimulus for larger families and was of itself highly controversial. These were the proposals for compulsory sex education in the schools (finally realized in 1956), for easy access to birth-control information and contraception, and for recognition of some "eugenic" and "humanitarian" as well as medical indications for abortion. Together with the law protecting women against loss of employment for marriage or pregnancy (a practice prevailing especially in private white-collar employment), an important principle was pinpointed: that women are not only mothers, and that population policy demands that their rights as individuals be protected rather than submerged in women's "duty to society."

With the introduction of voluntary unemployment and sickness insurance in 1934 and improved old-age and disability pensions insurance legislated in 1937, the foundations for a general minimum level of security were laid. This established the welfare-state policy of socialization of consumption rather than of production, beginning with services for children and gradually screening an increasingly large area of life from the play of the market. At the end of the forties a pension scheme ensuring everyone a basic pension regardless of paid employment was legislated, and in the fifties the national health-insurance plan was passed. A departure from original policy, which favored benefits in kind, was the introduction in 1948 of cash children's allowances for all children, justified on the grounds of rising food prices and the effect of inflation on other benefits. Most of these measures, particularly the basic pension, which provided at least a minimum of protection for women who had never worked outside the home, are implicit supports for greater economic independence for women.

The joining of Alva Myrdal's name with both the population program of the 1930s and the equality program of the 1960s is not fortuitous. One is tempted to classify the Myrdals, Alva and Gunnar, among Sweden's more important natural resources. They were among the first to realize that individual social measures have complex side effects and can cancel each other out if they are not part of a coordinated plan based on a conscious value system. From the beginning they were aware that social science is never really objective, and undermines itself by pretending to be so. Alva Myrdal wrote in 1940:

> To be truly rational, it is necessary to accept the obvious principle that a social program, like a practical judgment, is a conclusion based upon premises of values as well as upon facts.[12]

Other Nordic countries—Denmark, Norway, Iceland, and Finland —have developed broad social programs constructed along lines similar to Sweden's. In fact they cooperate closely, and since 1952 this cooperation has been coordinated by the Nordic Council. None of these countries has had as favorable conditions for social experiments as Sweden, however, and although all were influenced by the Myrdals' ideas, their efforts in the field of family policy were interrupted by the World War II, in which Sweden remained neutral.

These social supports are financed by a steeply progressive tax system. Sweden's claim to be the most "socialist" country in the Western world is based on the fact that the public sector receives a larger share of the GNP than it does in any other Western country, and employs more than one-third of the labor force. Sweden has a mixed economy in this sense, but to call it socialist is misleading. Walter Korpi's choice of "welfare capitalism" to describe his country's social system comes much closer to the mark.[13] Industry, trade, banking, and insurance remain in private hands to a greater degree than in Great Britain or Austria—countries where labor or Social Democratic governments have enjoyed much shorter stretches of power. State and local authorities own a controlling interest in nuclear power, and state-owned enterprises account for 70 percent of ore extraction in Sweden; in the other major industrial branches private firms are responsible for 97 percent of the payroll. State ownership has expanded primarily in the north, a huge, thinly populated, depressed area where the creation of new jobs is a serious problem. Swedish economist Tore Sellberg finds that private business has not been unduly oppressed by four decades of Social Democratic rule: "An international comparison discloses that the corporations make a rather modest contribution to direct tax revenues in Sweden."[14] While private firms contribute a sum equal to about 30 percent of total payroll (1976) in various forms of employee insurance premiums, and another 11 percent in paid holidays, they enjoy substantial benefits in the form of liberal depreciation rules on goods inventories, plant, and machinery. At least until the wave of strikes and lockouts that brought Swedish life almost to a halt in May 1980, losses due to strikes have been minimal in Sweden thanks to a 1938 agreement between the trade-union confederation and the employers outlawing strikes during the life of a union contract.

A larger proportion of Sweden's public revenues come from direct taxes on income and wealth than in any other European country. In 1975 the government recovered 51 percent of its GNP in direct taxes (83 percent) and social-security charges (17 percent), compared to 30 percent in the United States. One-third of this was returned to the public in the form of cash social payments, and two-thirds was used for public consumption and investments. Swedish citizens pay the highest income taxes in the world, and it is often suggested that the breaking point is close—as the highly publicized flight from Sweden of film director Ingmar Bergman, to escape tax penalties, dramatized. In 1975 the less-publicized average worker earning 40,000 Swedish crowns (at that time about $10,000) before deductions paid a tax of 34 percent; a university professor earning the equivalent of $25,000 paid 54 percent. As inflation raises incomes into higher tax brackets, the ranks of tax protesters increase.

What makes a country forgo other pleasures to finance a social-service program providing support for all its citizens in illness, old age, unemployment, and emergencies, and guaranteeing the basic needs of children? Aside from finding a connection between growth of social services and industrialization, international studies have failed to provide a clear answer. U.S. researchers Sheila B. Kamerman and Alfred J. Kahn sought connections between a country's characteristics and its social services, and found them impossible to pin down.[15] Another American authority, Harold Wilensky, identifies the age structure of the population (the percent of the population over 65) as the most important determinant in social-security system spending and believes there is a correlation between affluence and social-security outlays, with a tendency for spending for this purpose to level off over time at about 20–25 percent of GNP. He sees the age of the system to be another factor, as budget increases are usually expressed in percentage increments. A European, Kurt Bayer, takes issue with Wilensky, arguing that political systems play a significant role. "Early and persisting socialist and other workers' movements account for stronger reliance on willingness to engage in social service efforts," he writes. He adds that "in addition to the level of economic growth, the ideology prominent in the country has an important influence on the level of spending," pointing out that two of the world's richest countries, Switzerland and the United States, are welfare laggards.[16]

The comparison in Table 1 (see Appendix) seems to support all these arguments. One thing at any rate emerges clearly: with its high per capita GNP and high rate of spending, Sweden heads the list in absolute per capita expenditures on welfare. By 1976 direct social services accounted for nearly 25 percent of Swedish GNP. For many years Sweden has competed with Switzerland, and more recently Norway, for the top ranking in per capita income among the world's most industrialized countries in analyses by the Organization for Economic Cooperation and Development (OECD).

Attempts to express the standard of living or the quality of life in statistics inevitably give Sweden high marks. It has the highest life expectancy and the lowest infant mortality rate (see Table 2). Its rates of unemployment and of deaths in traffic accidents are among the lowest in the world, while its standards of housing, measured in persons per room and percentage of dwelling units with indoor plumbing, are again among the highest. Moreover, measured by per capita calorie intake over the recommended level, Swedes are less inclined than other wealthy nations to overeat. Using 25 such indicators in a cross-national study of 15 OECD countries, an Austrian investigator, Lore Scheer, has placed Sweden first in quality of life.[17] Any traveler to Sweden can observe that public spending has created a cushion of security, that public responsibility is taken for granted, and that social services are administered with respect for human dignity.

Equality, however, has continued to evade capture. By the late sixties, earlier illusions about the possibility of achieving a real redistribution of wealth or even a real reduction in income differences through full employment plus social policies directed particularly at the nonearning members of society, had evaporated. The basic minimum available to everyone had been increased by expanding services in kind and cash benefits from social insurance, but the actual gap between the well-off and the less well-off had widened.

It was realized, according to Per Holmberg, an economist and professor at the Stockholm Graduate School of Social Work and Public Administration, that the long-term results of social policies on equality had not been sufficiently studied, and that reforms are "as a rule founded primarily on hypotheses of a tentative and pragmatic nature."[18] While the equalizing impact of social-welfare policies was taking effect, there were new forms of inequality and insecurity arising which the policies of the 1930–50s did not, and were not designed to, address. The welfare state had eliminated destitution; the "new poverty" was relative, but real nonetheless. Between the 1940s and the early 1960s the income differential between blue- and white-collar workers increased, as did the differentials between various geographical areas and occupations and between women and men. Opportunities for advancement went to those who already had opportunities. Grants, loans, and tax advantages to private enterprises to stimulate employment increased the wealth gap. "Political poverty" was the expression coined to describe the situation of those low on the power scale who could not or did not make use of their rights.

The Social Democratic Party's Equality Program, adopted at its 1969 congress, marked, according to Holmberg, a reorientation toward political action to change people's economic and social situation. It recognized a conflict between the aim of achieving living conditions on the basis of need, and the operation of a labor market that concentrated on profits and productivity. Employment opportunities began to be seen as the most important factor in income differentials, and the labor market as the ground to which the battle for equality had to be transferred. A series of reports published by the government's Low Incomes Commission beginning in 1970 provided support for this argument, finding that "low incomes and underemployment were both widely diffused," and that "the redistribution of income under social policy was a system with no more than negligible redistributive effects."[19] Poverty, in short, was not being wiped out. Indeed, some critics charged that social policy was simply disguising the existence of poverty and thus reinforcing the system that produced it.

Victims of the "new poverty" included one-parent households and families with several children, as well as immigrant workers; poverty was found in families where there was no unemployment and no social aberration. Women were a substantial part of the new poor. In 1971, 16 percent of families with children under 18 were one-parent families, and of these better than 90 percent were headed by women. In industry the average monthly earnings of all women workers were 70 percent of men's, and those of women white-collar workers were 58 percent of men's. When all full-time white-collar employees were studied, women were found to earn 42 percent less than men in the private sector and 18 percent less in the public sector. It was this segregated job market that became the main focus of the sex-role equality drive.

Notes

1. "The Status of Women in Sweden: Report to the United Nations 1968," in Edmund Dahlström, ed., *The Changing Roles of Men and Women* (Boston: Beacon Press, 1971), p. 215.

2. "The Emancipation of Men: Karin Westman-Berg interviewed by Ying Toijer-Nilsson," *Herta* 2 (1975): 5.

3. Alva Myrdal and Viola Klein, *Women's Two Roles: Home and Work* (London: Routledge & Kegan Paul, 1966), p. 192.

4. Moberg is quoted in Rita Liljeström, "Sweden," in Sheila B. Kamerman and Alfred J. Kahn, eds., *Family Policy: Government and Families in Fourteen Countries* (New York: Columbia University Press, 1978), p. 33; Anna-Greta Leijon, *Swedish Women—Swedish Men* (Stockholm: The Swedish Institute, 1968), p. 149.

5. *Towards Equality: The Alva Myrdal Report to the Social Democratic Party* (Stockholm: Prisma, 1971), p. 82.

6. See Franklin D. Scott, *Sweden: The Nation's History* (Minneapolis: University of Minnesota Press, 1977), pp. 106-107, for discussion of this point.

7. Alva Myrdal, *Nation and Family* (Cambridge: MIT Press, 1968), p. 15.

8. Walter Korpi, *The Working Class in Welfare Capitalism* (London: Routledge & Kegan Paul, 1978), p. 72. Significantly, this important book contains but a handful of references to women.

9. Rita Liljeström, *A Study of Abortion in Sweden* (Stockholm: Allmänna Förlaget, 1974), p. 39.

10. A. Myrdal, *Nation and Family*, p. 28.

11. Ibid., p. xviii.

12. Ibid., pp. 1-2.

13. See Korpi, *Working Class in Welfare Capitalism*.

14. Tore Sellberg, "The Swedish Economy," in *Profile of Sweden* (Stockholm: The Swedish Institute, 1972), p. 165.

15. Alfred J. Kahn and Sheila B. Kamerman, *Social Services in International Perspective* (Washington, D.C.: U.S. Department of Health, Education, and Welfare, 1977), pp. 26-28.

16. Kurt Bayer, "Economic Conditions and Social Services in Europe, 1970-1975," *Eurosocial Occasional Papers*, No. 2 (Vienna: European Centre for Social Welfare Training and Research, 1976), pp. 8, 13. For Wilensky's investigation see Harold L. Wilensky, *The Welfare State and Equality: Structural and Ideological Roots of Public Expenditures* (Berkeley, Ca.: University of California Press, 1975).

17. Lore Scheer, "Conceptualizing the Quality of Life," *Labour and Society* 3, no. 1 (1978): 63-79.

18. Per Holmberg, "Introduction and Background," in *Swedish National Report to the Eighteenth International Conference on Social Welfare*, San Juan, Puerto Rico, *July 18-24*, 1976 (Stockholm, 1976), p. 6.

19. Rita Liljeström in Kamerman and Kahn, eds., *Family Policy*, p. 28.

CHAPTER 2

Attacking the Differences

The change in the pattern of women's employment in Sweden in the past twenty years has been nothing short of spectacular. In 1960 it was still the rule for married women to stay at home even after their children were grown. In Sweden the overall female labor-force participation rate slid downhill steadily after the age of 20, in contrast to the United States, where the curve began to rise to a second peak after 30 (see Figure 1, Appendix). As a Swedish economist, Siv Gustafsson, describes it: "The conditional equality attitude had conquered in the USA in 1960, whereas in Sweden the paternalistic attitude still dominated."[1] By 1975, however, Sweden's graph also showed a second peak at age 40–45, and the work-force participation rate for married women had risen to 67 percent, compared to 45 percent in the United States. Sweden had become the leader of the Western world as far as women's work outside the home was concerned (see Table 3) and was not far behind Eastern Europe.[2]

The economic expansion that followed World War II sent Swedish employers looking for workers. A continuously declining birthrate, the extension of compulsory schooling, and a shorter workday had all contributed to the diminishing labor reserve. As in other western European countries, employers preferred to hire "guest workers" from abroad, both because many of the jobs opening up were "male" and because immigrant men could be expected to be more mobile than Swedish women. Immigration, from Finland especially but from southern Europe as well, increased rapidly, and most of this foreign labor went into industry. Swedish trade unions, however, were anxious to limit competition from outsiders who might bring wage rates down, and their pressure, combined with awareness of the social problems created by mass immigration, persuaded the government to introduce stricter entry requirements for workers coming from outside the Scandinavian region (there is free migration among the Nordic Council countries, and in fact most immigrant workers in Sweden came from Finland). Between 1960 and 1970 women made up the total increase in the labor force; their numbers rose by nearly a quarter of a million while the male work force declined by 72,000. The percent of women with children under seven who were employed outside the home increased from 37 percent in 1965 to 57 percent in 1974. By the latter year women accounted for 41 percent of the work force; by the end of the decade the figure was 44 percent.

Once women became the preferred alternative to imported labor, and the chief source of new union members, the unions began to take an interest in measures to support women's work. The Joint Female Labor Council, which had been established in 1950 by the two large labor confederations (LO representing blue-collar workers and TCO speaking for the majority of salaried employees) and the Confederation of Swedish Employers (SAF) had the task of investigating women's conditions and publicizing the results. Under the impact of the equality debate, it identified the major causes of women's inequality at work as the unequal division of responsibilities in the home and the irrational prejudices of men and women concerning the division of occupations outside the home as well.

Increasingly impatient criticism from women calling for action on this hypothesis led to the replacement of the Joint Council in 1972 by the Advisory Council on Equality between Men and Women, appointed by Prime Minister Olof Palme and directly responsible to his office. The Advisory Council consisted of five active Social Democrats, all women. They could call on a consultative body of 20, representing the unions, the employers, several government agencies, county and municipal authorities, and all the major women's organizations, but the power to decide on recommendations to the government rested entirely with the council itself. The directives provided by the government were very general. The stress was on the right of women to employment "in the first place," and, the government's advice continued, "This means that the labor market policy and other public action to create employment, together with the regeneration of the conditions of working life, take precedence here."[3]

A powerful instrument for carrying out suggestions made by

the council and approved by the government already existed in the National Labor Market Board, the agency that implements labor-power policy and runs the public employment service consulted by 85 percent of all Swedish job seekers. Both labor and management are represented on the National and County Labor Boards and the District Employment Boards, although the majority of members are appointed by the government.

The agency's task, financed from the State Budget, is to maintain full employment through placement activities. It can initiate public works and approve government orders to private firms in order to defer shutdowns. To avoid layoffs it organizes an in-plant training system in cooperation with the National Board of Education, providing some 300 courses in 50 centers for job seekers, who receive grants while learning and are eligible for further funds to cover travel and relocation. Another of its duties is supervision of the deployment and training of labor power in firms making use of government grants and training subsidies under the regional development program. The board also approves the release of investment reserves to private firms under the government scheme giving tax deductions to companies that set aside a percentage of their profits to be used in recession periods. This service thus affects, in one way or another, directly or indirectly, most of Sweden's labor force of 1.86 million women and 2.37 million men. Consequently, when the Council on Equality between Men and Women started its work, the idea of measures to influence the structure of the labor force and to give special support to its weaker members was by no means new and did not appear as an invasion of anyone's liberties.

Moreover, two traditional obstacles to job equality between the sexes had already been weakened—protective legislation, and the hourly wage differential between men's and women's work.

The Scandinavian countries were the first to come to the conclusion that laws prohibiting the employment of women in certain jobs hurt women more than they help them and that labor legislation should be designed to protect *both* sexes. When in 1927 the International Trade Union Women's Conference expressed itself in favor of special protection for women workers, the Swedish and Danish delegates abstained. The first Swedish Social Democratic Women's Conference in 1907 had opposed a ban on night work for women, and while the regulation was introduced in spite of their objections, it was abrogated in 1962. None of the five Nordic countries signed the International Labor Organization (ILO) convention on night work or on the maximum weights women may be permitted to lift. Only Finland remains a signatory to the agreement prohibiting underground work for women; Sweden withdrew its signature in 1936.

Sweden signed the United Nations convention on equal pay in 1960, but the ineffectiveness of equal pay legislation in closing the male-female wage gap is no secret. A gradual reduction of the difference has taken place in Sweden as a result of the blue-collar unions' traditional "solidarity" wage policy, which for many years has given the lowest-paid workers a higher percentage wage increment in every national contract. Since most women in industry fall into this category, their average hourly earnings rose from 68.8 percent of men's in 1960 to 80 percent in 1970 and 87 percent in 1977. Like all averages, of course, this one conceals considerable differences between the actual earnings of individuals.

The Advisory Council gave wide publicity to the disadvantages women experienced in the segregated job market. The most frequently cited figures showed that in 1970, 72 percent of all gainfully employed women were concentrated in 25 occupations, all of them traditionally female and most of them connected with women's "caretaking" functions. Only 12 percent of all employed men worked in these jobs and, in contrast to women, men were distributed throughout nearly 300 occupations. In the civil service, where 42 percent of all employees were women, they were 76 percent of the lowest paid and only 2 percent of the staff at the top of the salary scale. In teaching, where women dominated, they still held only 9 percent of the highest-paid posts. Because of this distribution of jobs, and because so many women worked part-time, in 1972 the annual median earnings of gainfully employed women were 52 percent of men's.

The work of the council received extensive media coverage. Spokeswomen stressed the need for ending the division of the labor market into male and female sectors. Expressions like "measures to eradicate the differences" were freely used. Expectations were aroused that what was in the works was an all-out attack on the almost automatic selection of men for most jobs in industry and the better-paying positions elsewhere. While an energetic public-education campaign was mounted to make people think about how and why this selection process took place, however, the steps actually proposed had considerably more limited goals. Priority was "given to measures which strengthen the status of those women who are worst off with regard to education, training, employment and income, and who also lack all influence in society."[4]

Three measures of labor-market policy were proposed by the council and were incorporated in a law that took effect in 1974. According to this law:

—Labor Market Boards were to hire 100 employment officers who were to concentrate on placing women, and on maintaining contact with employers and unions for this purpose;

—Special training grants were to be paid to employers who trained women or men for certain occupations dominated by the opposite sex;

—Companies obtaining grants under the regional development scheme were enjoined to engage not less than 40 percent of either sex when taking on new workers.

Meanwhile, in the summer of 1973 an experimental program was launched in Kristianstad, one of Sweden's southernmost counties, with a population of 230,000, where the primarily male-oriented industries were having trouble finding men workers. Many women were registered as unemployed, and the potential for introducing women into traditional male industries seemed unusually high. It was the experience of Labor Market Board officials that most women did not want to work in industry, but as one of them said, "We thought if we could just get them to look at the inside of a factory they might be more interested." When the idea was first broached to employers they said, "Never!" As there seemed to be no alternative, however, several plant managers agreed to cooperate. They had nothing to lose, since the county employment service was prepared to find the women and pay for their training.

The first three projects undertaken between August 1973 and January 1974 involved the country's largest factory manufacturing sanitary porcelain, insulators, fuses and other electrical equipment; a plant making prefabricated houses; and a Saab-Scania factory producing engines and gear boxes for trucks. The county employment service extended a widely publicized invitation to all women to attend "information days" at the plants, designed to attract housewives and other women with little vocational training. Meanwhile "adjustment groups" in the plants, originally set up to facilitate the integration of the handicapped and the elderly, were given the task of deciding which jobs were to be tried by the women and of persuading the male workers that it was a good idea.

The women's travel expenses to the gathering were paid and day care was provided. Many more women attended than had been expected. Those who were convinced by what they saw and heard could attend a four-week "Working Life and Training" course during which they were able to try out as many jobs as they wanted. Some took the first one they tackled, others tested as many as eight or nine, some did not find any they liked. All received training grants while they were learning. By February 1975, fourteen firms in Kristianstad county were taking part in the project; 311 women had attended "information days," of whom 170 started courses and 123 were fitted to jobs. While the numbers may seem small, it must be remembered that a "large" plant in Sweden, like the sanitary porcelain factory in Kristianstad, has 1,000 employees. In the metal working industry, Sweden's largest, 98 percent of plants have less than 500 workers.

It was estimated that in addition to those women hired as a direct result of the project, another 400—500 women were taken on in Kristianstad as a side effect. National Labor Market Board officials were sufficiently interested in the results to extend the program to five more of Sweden's 24 counties.

Results on the whole were positive. Plants that had had previous experience with women workers had much less trouble absorbing more, especially if they joined in a group. The Orrefors Works in Kalmar county, Sweden's most up-to-date glass factory making fine crystal, had trained the first ten women glass cutters in the country ten years previously, and in 1975 six of them were still on the job. Four more were hired as part of the Kristianstad project. The plant also trained the first women glass blower in its own school. By 1975 about one-quarter of its workers were women and at the affiliated plant at Sandvik, 30 miles away, the figure was 35 percent.

At Kalmar's small shipyard, however, which took on six young women to be trained as welders, its first-ever female employees, both the young engineer speaking for management and the fatherly trade-union representative agreed that 'it's not a favorable industry for women.'' Pressed to be more specific, they acknowledged that theoretically women could learn all the jobs, but they believed that it would not be good for women to work out of doors, nor would they like the jobs that had to be done in cramped quarters and uncomfortable positions. They seemed particularly concerned that injuries received in shipbuilding might damage a girl's looks— as opposed to those that might be suffered in the textile industry, which were likely to be less visible. The young women themselves shared none of these opinions. They liked their jobs and had applied for them because there was no other full-time work available. They acknowledged, however, that once they had children they would probably look for part-time work, even though they took it for granted that their husbands would share family responsibilities with them.

One Kristianstad factory was sufficiently pleased with its new women workers to hire an ergonomist and a physical-training instructor, and it announced that half its jobs could be redesigned for women. In the small prefabricated-housing factory, however, which had never employed women before and took on only five, no one was satisfied. Payment was according to team output, and the women felt that the men expected more of them than they did of each other. Their presence seemed to provoke an exaggerated amount of sex talk. One woman was struck by the fact that the men never referred to their wives by name but as "the old woman" and sometimes "the old bitch." For its part, management complained that the women expected special treatment as a result of the pilot program and the equality drive.

What were the concrete gains of the Kristianstad project? It was officially announced that during the years 1973—76, as a direct consequence of the program, 2,000 women had been placed in jobs. One representative of the Labor Market Board said that the project resulted in a general increase in the hiring of women by industry, and that "all over Sweden employers have begun to change their minds." Indeed, there was a rise of 20,000 in the number of women employed in manufacturing between 1973 and 1975. In purely statistical terms, however, the increase brought the position of women in industry, both absolutely and percentagewise, only back up to the level of 1963—65, years of peak economic activity. The figure may, of course, disguise an improvement in job distribution and in consciousness of equality issues. If there was anyone in those years in Sweden who did not know what Kristianstad meant, it could only have been because they did not read the papers or watch TV. The young women who managed to handle heavy insulator parts without damaging them and to glaze washbasins and lift them to a conveyor belt, and the burly male workmates who said that at first they had been dubious but had discovered that women could (or sometimes could not) do their share, were good for endless human interest stories. Television programs turned up instructive examples of sexism on the part of interviewers as well as interviewees. Kristianstad brought real life from the factory floor into the discussions that climaxed in International Women's Year.

An in-depth study of 50 of the women who had found jobs through the pilot project and of their families, from the point of view of family sociology, was made at the request of the Advisory Council on Equality by a research group at the University of Göteborg headed by Rita Liljeström.[5] This report must have contributed to the new realism about the possibility of opening up men's jobs to women without first creating conditions that would break the restrictive patterns into which men and women are locked in every aspect of their lives.

The older married women, Liljeström's team found, valued their new jobs primarily because through them they broke out of their isolation and came into contact with the outside world. Lacking self-esteem as well as skills, these women were satisfied with their largely routine industrial tasks, and undemanding about their conditions. The work itself was not usually as monotonous as typical women's assembly-line employment, but it was dirty, noisy, repetitious, and often strenuous. The women undervalued the importance of their economic contribution to the family; there was an unspoken agreement between them and their husbands that the man was the breadwinner. It was, after all, his reason for living, his identity. In many instances the men worked in still heavier jobs than the women and were too exhausted to take over the care of the children, who sometimes seemed as mysterious to them as did the inside of a factory to the women. These families also tended to be suspicious of day care—when it was available.

Young women who had not yet experienced isolation as housewives and mothers were highly critical of the factory environment and the nature of the work. They would never have chosen it if they had not already disqualified themselves for other jobs by discontinuing their education. It was easy for them to think of having children and staying home for a while. The roles in these future families were already there in embryo.

One thing "Kristianstad" could not do was advance the desegregation of the labor market in any real sense, and it was not designed to do so, although many people seem to have thought that it was. Its purpose was to get the least qualified and most vulnerable unemployed women into the work force in a situation where they did not have to compete with men. As Joan McCrae, a U.S. economist, has commented: "This pilot program for preparing women to enter the work force is suitable when there is a labor shortage concurrent with a pool of unskilled labor. The coincidence that it is men's jobs and housewives' labor brings it into the arena of equality of the sexes."[6] In short, if men had been available, employers would not have gone along with the project.

The Labor Market Board thought well enough of the scheme to make it part of the repertoire of measures available to the employment service in all 24 counties, but it was not extensively used because economic recession largely eliminated the shortage of unskilled and semiskilled labor. Kristianstad did prove the worth of the "Working Life and Training" course, which is a permanent part of the employment service's vocational-training program. It is valuable for the orientation of uncertain and inexperienced job seekers, who derive support from being in a group of people who share their situation. It provides information, testing, and guidance, and a chance to try out several occupations or a number of jobs within a particular branch. Thus it is well designed for breaking down traditional occupational choices in individual cases, and has been used with success to introduce men into caretaking jobs. In 1977—78, of the 85,000 people who took part in vocational training run by the Labor Market Board with the Board of Education, 11,000 were enrolled in these special preparatory courses, of whom 65 percent were women.

Of the three general employment measures adopted at the Advisory Council's suggestion, only one had brought benefits. This was the use of quotas that bind firms seeking regional development support to recruit at least 40 percent of each sex for any new jobs created. Between 1974 and 1976, the proportion of women in such firms rose from 19 percent to 21 percent. The offer of grants to firms that took on and trained members of the "nontraditional" sex was hardly taken up; apparently the grants were too low. The assignment of 100 special placement officers to the local employment-service offices in order to push women's employment had the effect of encouraging other officials to shift all "women's questions" to these officers and otherwise to ignore the issue. These special positions have now been abolished and the problem of equality has been made a responsibility of every placement officer. An "equality group" at the national level and individuals at lower levels are now responsible for seeing that something actually happens. Berit Rollén, the National Labor Board director in charge of labor-market questions, told a conference in the United States in 1978: "... Equality is a facet of our daily work that has to be applied in every field at all times. . . . We are still having some difficulty getting this across to all the eight thousand members of our staff."[7]

The first half of the seventies was a period of experimentation in which the difficulties of influencing the conventional distribution of jobs between the sexes proved to be more formidable than was anticipated. There were overly optimistic expectations about what could be accomplished by the mere presence of women in areas staked out by men. The assumption was made that, in addition to paying more, men's jobs were intrinsically better than women's and that women would prefer them if their initial resistance could be overcome. But while it is true that men's jobs on the whole offer more variety, more responsibility, more prestige, and more upward mobility than do women's, this is not the case for the lowest jobs in industry, which require minimal skill and experience. Here the satisfactions, if any, lie in the congeniality of male work groups—to which, as Liljeström's study showed, women do not have easy access. Unless women can rise through further training, the effect of recruiting them to the least desirable jobs could be the creation of new badly paid "female" occupations.

Moreover, it is truly a case of swimming against the stream— and a stream with a strong current—to try to bring about a substantial invasion of the industrial labor force by women when that labor force is shrinking; the service sector is where jobs are to be had. Although the total labor force has increased since 1965, the number of people employed in industry in Sweden has been dropping steadily (as in most of Western Europe) due to rationalization and the transfer of some manufacturing to countries with lower labor costs. Moreover, in Sweden the consumer-goods industries, which favor women workers, have been shrinking faster than those specializing in capital goods. Metalworking now accounts for 43 percent of employment in the industrial sector, and expansion here takes place primarily in the skilled categories, for which women are rarely available. Women must still be encouraged to train for industry in one-factory towns where there are few other employment possibilities, but the government's view of developments as far ahead as 1983 anticipates that the net additions to the labor force will all be women, and that because of the nature of demand they will be absorbed without any change in the ratio between women and men in the industrial and public sectors.

Two events brought a shift of emphasis in the equality drive in the autumn of 1976. One was the defeat of the Social Democratic Party after 44 years in office. The Advisory Council on Equality, a partisan body operating at the level of the Prime Minister's office, was replaced by a parliamentary body, the National Committee on Equality between Men and Women, representing all five political parties (Conservative, Center, Liberal, Social Democratic, and Communist). What the new committee lost—the close relationship to the government that its predecessor enjoyed—it gained in a broader base from which to draw ideas.

The second event was the arrival in late 1976 of the economic recession, whose effects had been delayed and cushioned in Sweden by subsidies, training and recruitment grants, relief projects, and other measures. The recession intensified labor-force segregation. Women's share in manufacturing jobs dropped from 16.6 percent in 1975 to 15.7 percent in 1977. By September 1979 the overall unemployment rate was announced to be over 2 percent, with another 1.5 percent receiving labor-market training and an additional 1.5 percent in relief work. Women were 44 percent of the work force but 55 percent of the unemployed. Moreover, while latent unemployment among women is reported to have decreased by half since 1970, partly due to the availability of unemployment assistance for applicants not eligible for insurance benefits, it is still considered to be widespread. Although the number of women who took part in labor-market training increased steadily through the seventies, their participation in courses related to manufacturing slid from a high of 27 percent of the total enrollment in such courses in 1974 to 12 percent in 1977. Similarly, while relief work opportunities for women had been increased (to one-fifth of the total), services and nursing accounted for nearly two-thirds of the places.

If women are not to lose further ground in the shrinking but powerful sector where the nation's wealth is produced, and if women are ever to hold their own in the expanding services where they are to account for the net growth in employment, the emphasis in the future will have to be on upward mobility—something the Swedish equality effort has largely neglected until now, possibly because it was associated with the ambitions of educated middle-class women who could be expected to take care of themselves. So far two experimental projects have been launched in industry. The first, jointly sponsored by the Committee on Equality and the Volvo Works at Köping near Stockholm, provided tailor-made courses in theory and practice for 17 women production workers, and the effects on them and those in their environment are now being studied. The second pilot scheme was run by the National Labor Market Board in the town of Ludvika in central Sweden, where women with long experience in industry were given two years of technical training. This, too, is still being evaluated.

As the seventies drew to a close, two obstacles among others appeared to be inhibiting the more general improvement of women's status:

—the lack of effective measures ruling out discrimination by employers and requiring affirmative action;

—the growth of part-time work by women, which reduced the likelihood of their receiving further training and their eligibility for the better jobs.

A curiosity, in a country as equality-conscious as Sweden, has been the absence until 1979 of national legislation outlawing discrimination on the basis of sex. The trade unions have always opposed such a law because of their attachment to a tradition, established in the 1930s, that matters concerning the labor market were best settled by the parties concerned—the unions and the employers. Even though the parties concerned in this issue included women, who were not represented in the negotiating bodies on either side, this reasoning was honored while the Social Democratic Party was in power. In 1975, at the request of this government, the Advisory Committee on Equality had presented a report on a proposed antidiscrimination measure originating with the Liberal Party. Predictably, since all its members were Social Democrats, the committee strongly recommended that the government *not* introduce such a measure. No sooner had a new coalition government headed by the Center Party come to power, however, than it called on the recently formed all-party Committee on Equality to draft a proposal. This bill, which was put to a vote in 1979, ordered employers to abstain from sex discrimination, but at the same time made clear that "special treatment" whose purpose was to promote equality would be permitted. Indeed, the bill enjoined employers to take affirmative action, and created the post of "Equality Ombudsman" to hear complaints and try to bring about voluntary compliance. If his or her mediation efforts failed, an Equality Commission was to be empowered to issue injunctions. Because five Center Party men unexpectedly broke ranks and voted "no," together with a number of unregenerately antifeminist Conservatives, the bill failed. Instead, a substitute Social Democratic bill was adopted, which banned discrimination without requiring affirmative action and without establishing enforcement machinery. The final round, however, went to the supporters of affirmative action. At the insistence of Minister for Immigration and Equality Affairs Karin Andersson, a Center Party leader who took office late in 1979 and who had headed the committee that brought in the original proposal, the bill was reintroduced and passed in December 1979, with its teeth restored and took effect in 1980. The first Equality Ombudsman is a woman, District Judge Inga-Britt Törnell.

In the midst of the discussion that preceded the parliamentary debates, the union confederations and the employers' association took action which they hoped would forestall antidiscrimination legislation. In 1977 the blue-collar confederation, LO, and PTK, the TCO Federation of Salaried Employees in Industry and Services, signed separate equality agreements with SAF, the Swedish

Employers' Confederation, covering all workers employed by private firms. The agreements are similar in substance: they ban all forms of discrimination and call for measures to promote equality between the sexes. Equality provisions are to be incorporated in every collective agreement, and equality committees set up in every shop. Complaints will be handled by the usual grievance machinery and will go before the the Labor Court only if all else fails. The agreement signed by the salaried employees' union calls for a joint council to supervise the agreement and stimulate activities, while the LO agreement leaves the initiative to the local unions. The former also provides for positive discrimination for a transitional period to aid the underrepresented sex.

The intention of these voluntary labor-management pacts was to show that compulsory affirmative action and government interference, in the form of an equality commission or other enforcement body, was unnecessary. Two and a half years after the signing of these agreements, ten pilot projects were running in firms covered by the agreement with the white-collar federation, chiefly involving the analysis and redesign of the jobs of typists, secretaries, and other clerical staff. One involved a joint union-management course to change attitudes in the personnel department. A similar course was planned for trade-union officials. No projects whatsoever were reported under the SAF-LO agreement covering blue-collar workers. These results, suggesting that in the private sector the unions and the companies were marking time, actually helped the passage of the antidiscrimination law. "As yet only isolated activities can be discerned aimed at meeting the requirements of the agreements," the Swedish government reported to a seminar held by the United Nations Economic Commission for Europe (ECE) in March 1979.[8]

The experience of the Swedish cooperative movement shows how hard it is to advance from the stage of agreements at the top and sonorous phrases that do not hurt anyone, to action. The Cooperative Union and Wholesale Society has 1.9 million members in 157 coop retail societies. Cooperatives account for about 5 percent of industrial production, an important sector of the food industry, and about 20 percent of retail trade. The consumer cooperative movement employs some 90,000 people in its purchasing departments, factories, warehouses, and retail outlets.

Under pressure from members, an "Equality Delegation" was

appointed in 1977 on the decision of the Cooperative Union's National Assembly, which agreed that the movement should be "a pioneer in the work for equality."[9] Nineteen seventy-nine was supposed to be a year of transition from the stage of surveys to practical, concrete measures. "Other companies and unions are turning to us for suggestions and experience," reports Bo Kjellberg, secretary to the Equality Delegation, whose job it is to convince the individual cooperative societies and their associated companies to set up their own equality groups, and who also helps initiate experiments in training and recruiting. All this work is carried out on the basis of agreements between the Cooperative Employers' Association and the unions.

Some 15 large cooperative societies representing about 70 percent of all coop employees had set up equality groups by the end of the year. "We have had to fight the attitude, common among both women and men important in the organization, that equality is important but that no special program is necessary," says Kjellberg. "They think it's automatic, it's coming, it may take a long time but it must take a long time, and we can't do anything if the schools and the home don't do it."

The cooperatives' Equality Delegation has established as a first principle that every workplace must have its own program, growing out of its specific situation, and with clear specific targets that everyone can grasp—"even if it takes two years to work it out." Essential parts of every program are

—an inquiry into the actual status of the employees;

—definite proposals for training, recruiting, and changing attitudes;

—getting the information back to everyone in the enterprise: "let women talk to the women, let management persuade management";

—fix responsibility: give everyone—the head of personnel, the head of in-plant training, etc.—specific tasks, and ask each for a personal accounting.

Everyone is very happy while making inquiries and writing up programs. Then comes the stage known as "facing reality," which according to Kjellberg is "very very painful." "Managers don't want ideology. They have to be shown that if they work for women, who are half the employees, it will be good for business," he says. A cooperative company making autoparts has started to train women as tire-builders with good results, but this has involved changing working conditions as well as designing special training. "It's a sign of women's good sense that they don't accept jobs under the conditions in which men work."

Two major findings that have come out of this early experience are that the system of recruiting people for better jobs is "definitely wrong" and that in-plant training has to be changed. Training and personal development should be discussed personally with each employee once a year, according to Kjellberg.

> Women between the ages of 20 and 30 are going to say *no* to further training because they have small children. It's very sad, of course, that men don't say *no* at that age too. Careers have to be available for women at age 40 or 45. They still have 20 good years left. But older women see young boys go into training courses and they think that they are too old and can never make it. You have to give education in self-confidence.

One such experimental course for "People Who Had Previously Said No to Further Training," has been tried out at the cooperative movement's central training college. Twenty women aged around 40, most of them part-time workers, took part in a series of lectures and discussions that also involved working out their personal programs for the future. Called together eight months after the conclusion of the course, they reported that it had been the best week of their lives. One woman had left her job to go back to school; most had asked for better jobs and some had taken on full-time work. This course is being repeated and one major cooperative society has arranged one of its own.

In the Civil Service—which employs as many women as does the shop floor in industry—activity started slowly after a government report in 1975 pinpointed numerous inequities in the system. The report gave "no support whatsoever to the belief that the existing differences would disappear, or even diminish substantially, solely because the agencies do not discriminate. . . ."[10] A government Equality Ordinance issued in 1976 called on every government agency to take steps to break down the division between men and women, and to make further training and promotion available to both sexes on equal terms. It requires the agencies to present annual reports on what they have done and what they intend to do.

Responsibility for coordinating the equality program rests with the Division for Personnel Affairs of the Ministry of the Budget. The ministry has no coercive powers, since Swedish government agencies enjoy a high degree of independence. "If the agencies don't follow the decree we can't do anything about it except write an angry letter," as Conny von der Capellen, who works with equality questions in the ministry, put it. Having acquired several volumes of reports from the agencies, the small ministry department dedicated to changing government practices has identified two general impediments to the upgrading of women. One is the way job requirements are formulated, and the other is the weight given to the qualifications people already have.

In describing a post for which applicants are being considered, the qualifications asked for are often unnecessarily high and tend to frighten women off. For example, university degrees will be specified even when a person with work experience and some courses in the field could do the job just as well. Moreover, a biased and inappropriate system of values underlies the granting of credits for experience. While military experience is considered a plus toward promotion in the law courts, a lifetime of dealing with children in the home is not. Applicants for executive jobs are given no credit for the ability to type—a skill that might well be required for most administrators. Such a policy would, of course, give most women an edge over most men.

Ten government agencies have recently been applying this thinking in an effort to get more women into top-ranking jobs. This has involved the rewriting of job descriptions to include relevant practical skills that women might have and to eliminate needlessly high demands. Jobs have been redesigned to avoid overtime or to permit a part-time work schedule. In the first experimental period, half the jobs for which women applied were actually filled by women—but women applied for only 50 percent of the openings. This has led to a change in the merit system that will allow more women to rise to middle-level positions, from which they can aspire to high-ranking vacancies.

Another group of government agencies has begun to hire women for what were traditionally men's jobs, and vice versa. The National Telecommunications Association has been actively seeking women for installation, repair, and line-maintenance work, and men for positions as telephone operators, salespeople, and cataloguers. No quotas were set, but weight was given to the applicant's sex. In the experimental period, 28 percent of those hired or transferred were of the "unconventional" sex, with women actively applying for men's jobs and men taking women's jobs because these happened to be available. When it came to evaluating satisfaction, the women were found to be much happier with their work than the men.

All reports from the numerous bodies in any way concerned with equality between the sexes point to the handicap represented by the large and growing proportion of Swedish women who work less than 35 hours a week (a 40-hour week has been in force in Sweden since 1972). The figure has increased from one-third of all gainfully employed women in 1974 to 45 percent in 1978, compared to 5 percent of men. Whereas earlier it was chiefly older women who chose part-time work, since 1974 most of the increment has been among women between the ages of 24 and 34.

One out of two employees in the public sector works part time, compared to one out of seven in manufacturing. Most of those who put in a short week are saleswomen, nurses' assistants, clerical workers, cleaners, janitors, and home helpers attached to municipal social-welfare departments. Their jobs are characterized by irregular schedules often involving evening or weekend work, and low social-security benefits. Part-time jobs are usually dead-end jobs, and the trade unions are reluctant to exert themselves for the people who fill them.

In view of these disadvantages, it has been hard for those who are pressing for equality to understand why women appear to be leaving full-time for part-time work instead of demanding training for better jobs. The unequal division of tasks in the home and the shortage of day-care places are the explanations most frequently given.

Yet from another point of view the popularity of part-time work among women helps to demystify the question of why women seem reluctant to take men's jobs. An analysis of part-time work as a positive statement of work preferences has emerged from a study conducted for the trade unions at the Center for Working Life, a recently established state-supported research institute, by a young economist, Marianne Pettersson.[11] It is based on the actual flow of women into and out of part-time work over time, with separate classifications for those who change their status more than once. Using data on 58,000 women compiled by the Central Bureau of Statistics, Pettersson compared the figures for six two-year periods between 1970 and 1977. She found that part-time and full-time work had *both* increased, while women who stayed outside the labor market entirely had dropped from a quarter to one-fifth of the total. Only a small percentage had shifted from full-time to part-time work, and these were balanced by an almost equal percent who moved the other way. The number who left their jobs to stay at home had decreased.

Pettersson concludes that the increase in part-time work by women is not to be attributed to a general withdrawal from full-time employment, but rather that more and more women are taking on short-time employment instead of remaining at home. This is particularly clear when the figures are broken down by age and number of children. Young women with a small child now work part-time instead of giving up work as they used to, and they remain steadily in part-time work when a second child is born. More women also continue to work full time after their first child is born.

Another conclusion from the study is that part-time work is not necessarily a consequence of lack of day-care facilities. On the contrary, it may be due to the availability of day care, since it is "long" part-time work (20–35 hours) that has increased. This suggests that parents simply do not want to have their children in day care for ten hours a day. While acknowledging all the objective disadvantages that part-time workers experience, Pettersson argues on the basis of interviews conducted for the project that many women consider a job with shorter hours an improvement in their living standard, while they would not feel that way about a full day of work outside the home. Also, many women consider their "caretaker" jobs meaningful, and prefer them to working under conditions that men accept only because it is not considered "manly" to complain about health and safety hazards. Like Bo Kjellberg of the Cooperative Union, she considers these women's reservations positive. Indeed, she says, "women's timidity should be upgraded."

The fact that the average number of hours worked by all women has dropped from 33 in 1970 to 31 in 1978 can be understood as a vote for the 30-hour week. The demand for the six-hour day was first put forward by the national organization of Social

Democratic women in 1972. Since then it has become widely recognized as an essential condition for a fairer division of responsibilities in the home. Its achievement depends, however, on the willingness of the trade unions to fight for it, and although the union confederations, along with the most of the political parties, have incorporated it in their long-term programs, their hearts belong elsewhere. "We don't have the unions with us," says a spokesperson for the Committee on Equality. In the view of the committee, the six-hour day is a key demand for women, but to labor leaders it is an unrealistic one, incompatible with the fight to keep wages ahead of inflation. Nothing underlines the difficulty of fitting women's needs into the traditional concept of industrial struggle better than the apparent conflict between these priorities.

At the beginning of the 1970s the goal in Sweden was still to establish the right of women to work, regardless of their family status. At the end of the ten-year period more than 70 percent of all women between ages 16 and 64 were gainfully employed. During the decade women made numerous small gains in terms of narrowing the pay differential and of opportunities for vocational training. Housewives could qualify for unemployment benefits. Equality programs proliferated, on paper at least. A variety of pilot programs were launched that could bear fruit if they were to be applied on a large scale. Almost no change took place in the distribution of women and men in employment, however (see Table 4). In fact, thanks to the increase in female employment and the shift in demand for labor from industry to the service sector, by mid-decade Sweden's work force had become one of the most highly segregated in Europe (see Table 5). The question still to be answered was how to attack this stubborn division of the job market into typically "male" and "female" occupations.

The search for an answer now went deeper. Following the defeat of the Social Democratic Party in the 1976 elections the cause of equality had ceased to be identified with a particular party. Women who were active in the various parties and in the trade unions began to identify aims held in common and to move away from their male counterparts. At the central level, the Committee on Equality now represented the whole spectrum of political views. Its head was a former secretary of the Center Party's women's organization, Karin Andersson. The vice-chairperson was Liberal Party MP Karin Ahrland, a former president of the Fredrika Bremer Association. The members included a former Social Democratic Minister of Labor, Anna-Greta Leijon, who had chaired the Advisory Committee on Equality under the Social Democratic government. While still stressing measures to integrate women into the male labor force, the committee was asking parliament and the public to think more about a different concept of working life. Its stand, as expressed in the previously mentioned Swedish government report to the ECE, in 1979, is that:

> Most of the work which has been done so far has focused on the transformation of the woman's role. It will be harder to get further now without even more intensive efforts to *transform the role of the man.* Public opinion, parental leave and the additional demands arising when a woman works are not enough to break the sex-role pattern. . . . Performance and career requirements at work will have to be reduced. . . . What is called for is a work organization in which human needs are the prime consideration.[12]

If at the end of the seventies women were not calling for change in the vigorous way they had at the start, it was not necessarily because they had become passive. The projects and investigations carried out in past years had highlighted a number of facts: women possessed qualifications that were different from men's and had so far been underrated; women often did not fit into the job-training schemes that had been devised for men; women rated jobs differently and did not accept the male working environment unquestioningly. Thus, while women were overwhelmingly in favor of work outside the home—of 7,000 women sampled by the Committee on Equality, only 10 percent preferred domesticity—they brought to the workplace criteria that differed from men's. Moreover, they were no longer prepared to do *two* full jobs. These explanations for women's behavior began to gain recognition.

By the close of the decade women had acquired two routes through which discrimination on the job could be fought—the union-employer agreements and the anti-discrimination law—although it was by no means clear how effective either would be. The controversy over legally prescribed affirmative action, like the preference of the unions for wage increases over a shorter work day, had dramatized some differences of interest between women workers and the representatives of organized labor that had not been so apparent when equality was still in the talking stage.

Notes

1. Siv Gustafsson, "Life Time Patterns of Labor Force Participation" (Paper presented at the meeting of Scandinavian Economists, Helsingør, Denmark, June 1-4, 1979), p. 12.

2. "Equal Opportunities for Women," in *The OECD Observer* 97 (1979): 28.

3. "Advisory Council to the Prime Minister on Equality between Men and Women, Sweden" (Document issued by the Advisory Council in Stockholm, n.d.), p. 1.

4. Anna-Greta Leijon, "Sexual Equality in the Labour Market: Some Experiences and Views of the Nordic Countries," *International Labour Review*, 1975, nos. 2/3, pp. 109-10.

5. Rita Liljeström, Gunilla Fürst Mellström, and Gillan Liljeström Svensson, *Roles in Transition* (Stockholm: Liber Förlag, 1978). A detailed description of the Kristianstad project may also be found in an earlier publication by the same authors, *Sex Roles in Transition* (Stockholm: The Swedish Institute, 1975).

6. Joan M. McCrae, "Swedish Labour Market Policy for Women," *Labour and Society*, 1977, no. 4, p. 398. A follow-up study by the same author appeared as "Equality of the Sexes in Sweden Under a New Government," *Labour and Society*, 1979, no. 3, pp. 309-24.

7. Berit Rollén, "Equality on the Labor Market Between Men and Women: A Task for the National Labor Market Board," in Ronnie Steinberg Ratner, ed., *Equal Employment Policy for Women: Strategies for Implementation in the United States, Canada and Western Europe* (Philadelphia: Temple University Press, 1980), p. 188.

8. "Report from the Swedish Government to the ECE seminar on the participation of women in the economic evolution of the ECE region" (Stockholm, March 1979), p. 11.

9. "Report on the Work for Equality Between Men and Women," *KF International Department Information* No. 96 227 (Stockholm: KF, International Department, July 1979), p. 1.

10. Bo Kjellberg, "Women in Government Service," *Current Sweden* 79 (1975): 6.

11. Marianne Pettersson, "Förändringar i den kvinnliga sysselsättningen i Sverige 1970-77 med särskild inriktning på deltidsarbetet." Report prepared for the Swedish Center for Working Life, Stockholm, 1979.

12. "Report from the Swedish Government to the ECE seminar," pp. 17-18.

CHAPTER 3

The Unions on the Equality Bandwagon

An exhibition called "The Right to be Human" had its inaugural showing under trade-union sponsorship in a large Stockholm factory in February 1975, as part of the activities launching International Women's Year in Sweden. Prime Minister Olof Palme was among those present. The exhibition's message was that imprisonment in the masculine role is at least as great a problem to men as conformity to a feminine ideal is to women; that a debate on liberation and equality must be about how men as well as women are forced to act out socially determined stereotypes. In short, its point was that men and women have the same battle to fight: for the right to be human. Photographs and documentary material mounted on mobile panels depicted the pressure on men to be aggressive and competitive, to keep a stiff upper lip, and to conquer new lands—both literally and figuratively. The alternative was shown too: that men like women could be allowed to be soft and kind, needed to be able to express emotion, and had a right to a share in parenting and in family life.

Commissioned by the Advisory Council on Equality between Men and Women (two of whose six members represented Sweden's two major union confederations with nearly three million members, LO and TCO), the exhibition was duplicated in offices, schools, factories, and public buildings throughout the country. It was based on a book of the same title by a woman and two men who had interviewed 70 men representing all types of occupations and every type of community. The authors had tried to discover the subjective feelings of these men about the way the world expected them to act and react. "Emotional solitude" was the description that fit the inner environment of most of the subjects. In spite of the male camaraderie and solidarity that men enjoy, only four of these men admitted to having a friend (apart from their wife) with whom they could discuss personal problems. Unwilling-ness to betray fear or anxiety was a characteristic of almost all. If they could not meet the expectations placed on them to succeed, and very often they could not, what was left to them?

The book *The Right to be Human*, accompanied by discussion material on the roles of men and women, became the focus of thousands of study circles and discussions during 1975. As co-sponsors of the campaign, the trade unions circulated it through their network of union courses and schools. Trade unionists were to take the lead in spreading the new view of equality—the shar-ing of roles and responsibilities by men and women.

The Central Organization of Salaried Employees (TCO), with about 950,000 members in 24 affiliated unions, began to run a course in family policy at its central residential school at Bergendal outside Stockholm, beautifully located at the water's edge and sur-rounded by pine trees. Designed for activists and paid members of union staffs, this course lasted a week and went deeply into legal, labor-market, social-security, educational, and consumer questions as they related to the development of the family and the division of tasks within it. The 25 participants were civil servants, teachers, white-collar workers in industry and the services.

Continuing the debate in a smaller group after one such session, a woman schoolteacher declared: "One thing we found out is that we are not the typical Swede: we wanted to come here, and we wanted to discuss these things." The others agreed that despite the fact that the equality program had already reached such an advanced legislative level, it was still a matter of indiffer-ence to many, perhaps most people. "Of course it's easy to say 'yes, I agree, things should be that way,' but for himself the indi-vidual Swede wants his wife at home, and the individual local councilman prefers wives who stay at home to spending his budget on day care," offered another speaker. Academic-type men might try the parental leave (offered to fathers as well as mothers of new babies for the first time in 1974), but "ordinary workers can't do it. They think people would laugh at them, and that's the reality, too."

"It's sort of heavy work going out with this idea. You can't let yourself get tired. You must continue and continue. Even if you can convince a small percentage, it's going in the right direc-tion" (Bengt, a draftsman).

"They are only interested in getting more money. Not in getting involved in these questions" (Lars, a statistician).

The key problem was seen as the need to mobilize women members. "They complain, but when it comes to putting forward our demands it's the men who make the decisions" (Marianne, a teacher).

"You can't say that it's particularly difficult to work with the family program because our difficulty is to interest women *or* men in *any* kind of trade-union activity. They belong, but they don't want to go to meetings—talk, talk, talk" (Marianne).

"It can't be right that men decide about what women want. They *have* to be more active. But they haven't got the time. That's why we want the six-hour day" (Ilse).

In another, more luxurious residential trade-union school in Hasseludden, another suburb of Stockholm, a group of younger blue-collar unionists was attending a course for activists run by LO. While at the TCO course participation was divided fairly evenly between men and women, here it was overwhelmingly male.

James (a worker in a paint factory): "When I work eight or ten hours a day and come home tired I just want something hot on the table and to sit and read the newspaper. OK, I'm being drastic, but that's the way it is in the average family. I agree it's wrong. What shall we do?"

Lars (a building worker): "I must say I never met a girl who would tolerate such a conservative attitude."

Nils-Arne (a male nurse in a psychiatric hospital): "I like to come home to a clean house where I can see that my wife has done a lot of things for our kids, for our comfort. In the same way, when my wife is working I do the same thing when I'm home. I make something special to eat. I put candles on the table."

The argument turned to whether women, unlike men, should have the right to choose between housework and a paid job.

Lars: "I'll never understand why only the woman should have the right to choose—because the woman I'm living with, if she should choose, it could mean economic disaster. She's earning about 250 dollars a month more than me. She's a computer operator."

James: "You didn't understand me. My wife is a psychologist. She was out of a job for three years. Then a job came up a long way from where we lived. It meant giving up the flat and now I have to commute to work. But I respect her right to choose. She studied eight years."

Mogen (a food-warehouse supervisor): "Swedish men are a lot more conservative than this discussion is trying to make out. The majority think a woman's first duty is to her husband and second to her family. I think we are naive to believe that if we work only six hours a day we will have two more hours to spend with our children. Most people will go on like they are doing today. Some will take a second job, and some will go fishing or give more time to other activities."

Lars: "You wouldn't like to spend more time with your children?"

Mogen: "Yes, I would, but I don't think the majority of men are willing to do that. You forget that if I stayed home for six months my company would find it very difficult to accept, but if my wife stays home that's natural. It doesn't work the other way around."

The exchange ended with general agreement that the main barrier to change—that is, to a more equal division of roles between men and women—was the attitude of employers, since they benefited from maintaining women as a poorly paid labor reserve. These workers did not raise the question of whether the attitudes they had described within their own labor organization might not be an equally strong barrier.

The historic reluctance of trade unions to take up the rights of women is too well known to need elaborate documentation. It had its beginnings in the justified fears of male workers that the moment they let down their guard, obedient and apathetic women workers would be introduced into industry after industry to do "men's work" at half the wages. The increasing sophistication of what the West German labor historian Werner Thönnessen calls "proletarian antifeminism"[1] can be traced in all the countries of the Industrial Revolution, progressing from protest meetings of male workers against the employment of women, through refusal to accept women as union members, insistence on lower wage categories for women tied to their supposed need to be protected from heavy work, down to present lip service in the cause of equality. Even socialist trade unions, allied to parties proclaiming the emancipation of women as one of their aims, have successfully subordinated women's demands to all their other political and economic goals, as Thönnessen has shown in the case of Germany between 1863 and 1933.

The present women's movement may represent the first real threat to male dominance of the labor movement, even though the danger at present is more implicit than actual. At the first international symposium devoted to women's problems on the industrial labor market and in its decision-making institutions, held in Vienna in 1978 and cosponsored by the Austrian Government and the ILO-affiliated International Institute for Labor Studies, it was suggested

> that the industrialized countries are witnessing a change in the demands of women who are now looking towards the unions for solutions to their work-related problems which lie within their [i.e., the unions'] sphere of competence. While for the moment this is acting as an incentive towards their unionization it was also noted that women's adherence to the unions was still somewhat conditional and that if the present male-dominated power structures were not sufficiently receptive and responsive to the special needs of women at the present time, it was possible that women would be constrained to find their own solutions autonomously through parallel (and possibly even rival) organizations.[2]

Alice Cook, a U.S. authority on industrial relations, has found unions in Great Britain, West Germany, Austria, and Sweden all haunted by this new spectre of woman power. In a report on a cross-national study which she gave at this same Vienna meeting, she said:

> There is no question that [the unions] have been greatly influenced by the rise of the women's movement over the past ten years in every country and by the attention governments and international bodies have given to all these matters. Although some unions may properly be accused of being the last to get on the equality trolley, they are all in effect on board.[3]

There is nothing obvious in the early history of Swedish trade unions that would explain why they were not the last but among the first to jump on the bandwagon, and have even helped to write the music for the band. They have put their organizational strength, officially at least, behind a new concept of the future in which the sexes are to play equally important roles in both public and private life. It is a fact that without their active support, few of the programs adopted in Sweden since 1968 that point in the direction of equality would have been possible.

Sweden's late industrialization meant that its unions came upon the scene when working men's initial fierce opposition to women's employment was ebbing in the industrializing countries on the European continent. The need to organize women was already being accepted. Sweden's first trade-union federations were founded in 1886, followed three years later by the establishment, with union backing, of the Social Democratic Labor Party. The Swedish Trade-Union Confederation (LO) was not created until 1898; up to then the party functioned as the unions' central board. From the very first, the growth of unionism has been closely connected with the development of labor's own political party. Although LO unions are not required to affiliate with the party, this symbiosis has remained the characteristic feature of Swedish labor history for more than 80 years.

The year the Swedish Social Democratic Party was born, 1889, was also the year when Clara Zetkin, the acknowledged spokesperson for women in the international Social Democratic movement, convinced the International Workers' Congress in Paris to support women's right to work because only work could bring women economic independence. The congress put it on the record that "male workers have a duty to take women into their ranks on a basis of equal rights," and demanded "in principle equal pay for equal work for the workers of both sexes. . . ."[4] Two years later in Erfurt, the German Social Democratic Party conference for the first time demanded universal suffrage without regard to sex, the abolition of all laws that discriminated against women, and free education for girls as well as boys.

Thus, it was not any particular Swedish virtue that caused the Social Democratic Party—which drew its inspiration from developments on the continent—to include equal voting rights for women and men in its first program. Furthermore, Sweden did not push particularly hard for the suffrage cause. Women in all the other Scandinavian countries had won full political rights before World War I (Finland in 1905, Denmark and Norway in 1915), while Sweden did not give women the vote until 1919.

As they did in other countries, women workers in Sweden at first formed their own trade unions. In 1909 the Women's Trade-Union Federation affiliated with LO. Females did not represent a force worthy of much notice, however, since during the entire pre-World War I period they never amounted to more than 10 percent of trade-union membership and, moreover, did not possess a political voice. As Swedish labor historian Gunnar Qvist describes the situation, "Traditions, prejudices, internal and external resistance and organizational lethargy led the LO to concentrate its efforts during this period on the problem of male employees and to limit its concern for women to a few feeble pronouncements on the principle of equal wages."[5] One of those feeble pronouncements was a formal statement in support of equal pay, adopted in 1909.

During the 1930s and early forties, while employment of women stagnated overall, the percentage of low-income women recruited by LO increased, bringing female membership up to 17 percent. The higher proportion of married women now employed created new problems on the labor market which became issues for the unions as well as the party. As discussed in Chapter 1, the thirties were, under the leadership of the Social Democrats, a period of intense legislative activity to secure full employment and greater security for labor—including social benefits that improved the position of women, among them equal pension rights, paid maternity leave, and the prohibition of dismissal on grounds of marriage or pregnancy. As the Social Democratic Party (ruling in coalition with the Agrarian Party) was the political voice of the labor movement, the unions were obviously involved in developing and supporting this program.

This did not stimulate the unions' militancy on behalf of their women members, however. In 1931 the LO Congress had rejected a motion calling for the prohibition of employment of married women in the state sector, but it refused to take a stand on the incidents of discrimination against married women that were brought to light by women delegates. On the question of equal pay, Qvist comments that although the ILO, founded in 1919 with Swedish participation, had the achievement of equal pay as one of its fundamental aims, everywhere "the equal wages for equal work clause remained a dead issue during the period between the two wars." The Swedish Social Democratic Party did not incorporate it in its program until 1944. "The question was avoided as much as possible among the union and political leadership of the Swedish labor movement."[6]

The advances that have taken place since World War II have been more the result of external influences than of a change of heart in the ranks of labor. The surge of support for principles of equality which accompanied the Allied victory over fascism in 1945 was reflected at the international level in the postwar work of ILO, which finally adopted a Convention on Equal Pay in 1951. In Sweden there was competition for new union members, and particularly women members, due to the parallel expansion of white-collar unionization and female employment. The white-collar unions formed their own confederation, the TCO, in 1944, and very soon began to talk about equal pay and equal employment opportunities. TCO women were in a better position to put forward their demands because of their greater representation and their higher level of education. (According to a study of full-time unionized workers in 1974, 82 percent of LO women were manual workers, while 89 percent of TCO women were classified as "lower middle class," suggesting more articulate women with skills, and thus a better bargaining position.) Not committed to any political party, these unions represented a potential political counterweight as well.

Under the pressure of this competition, LO created a Women's Council in 1947. Like such bodies elsewhere, however, this was only an advisory committee. It would transmit upward from the ranks proposals which were then considered and voted upon by male executives, boards, and delegates. LO also decided to press for equal pay and thus initiated its successful "solidarity" wage policy, which raised women's pay by giving higher percentage increases to the lowest wage categories. Nevertheless, separate pay scales for men and women continued to be written into contracts negotiated by LO and its member unions until 1960. Only when this practice was discontinued did Sweden ratify the ILO Convention on Equal Pay.

Despite this less than distinguished record, in comparison to the male-dominated blue-collar union organizations in other countries the Swedish LO was relatively quick to recognize that women were coming to the fore with new demands, that they would not be satisfied indefinitely with token concessions, and that if existing organizations did not satisfy them they would go elsewhere. Clearly one good reason for this is LO's acute political sensitivity, arising from its close identity with a party that has long commanded the support of more than 40 percent of the country's electorate, undisturbed by world wars and the strong political disagreements that have weakened the unity of the labor movement elsewhere. Since the 1960s, TCO and LO have cooperated amicably and they take similar positions on most labor issues.

Added to this, LO, like the party itself, has been under pressure from the Social Democratic women's association, which, thanks to the party's record in the field of social policy, has attracted over the decades the majority of active and socially committed women with a left-of-center political orientation.

In turn, the Social Democratic women have felt the pressure of a growing feminist sentiment among younger women, particularly students and intellectuals, outside the established political machinery. Many of them joined or cooperated with a new leftist-feminist organization called Group 8, founded in 1968, which took women's issues out of the inner sanctums and into the streets. Women who were impatient with how slowly things moved on the local level, who felt powerless in the official Social Democratic structure, who wanted to discuss the sexual exploitation of women in terms considered offensive and threatening in Social Democratic women's clubs, organized in informal groups and even made contact with women in factories to try to interest them in cooperating on issues like part-time work, the shorter workday, and day care. Sweden had before it the example of Norway and Denmark, where feminist organizations had made serious inroads on the Social Democratic vote. Membership in the Swedish Social Democratic women's federation also suffered, dropping from 68,000 in the early sixties to 60,000 in 1968 and 45,000 in 1975.

LO reacted. Its Women's Council was transformed into a Council for Family Affairs composed of six women and five men representing the eleven largest national unions. In 1969 the council's report, which echoed the Social Democratic Party's Equality Program of 1968, became the basis for LO's goals in the area of sex-role equality. These were still expressed very cautiously, in terms of a general policy of priority treatment for underprivileged groups. Nevertheless, the blue-collar unions' stated targets included allocation of jobs without regard to gender, expansion of day care, individual taxation, social-security benefits keyed to the individual without regard to sex or marital status, and the reform of education to break down stereotyped ideas about what was appropriate for men and women.

TCO was much more outspoken when it adopted its family policy reform program in 1973. All adult family members, TCO declared, should have the same opportunity of being gainfully employed and all work in the home should be divided equally between men and women. The unions were called upon to play an active part in enforcing these ideas in practice. Legislation and social and educational policies that would contribute to sex-role equality were outlined. In a statement distributed in 1975, TCO castigated both private and public employers for their discriminatory employment policies and for discouraging their male employees from taking advantage of their legal right to parental leave. "The lip service to equality that was so characteristic of the sixties is no longer enough," it said. "The seventies must be a decade of action."[7]

Since then both confederations have made new family policy statements, much more detailed and much more militant in formulation. The report adopted at LO's 1976 congress "demands equality of the sexes in the labor market." It proposes numerous reforms in education to influence pupils in the direction of unconventional choices; it calls on all affiliated unions to cooperate in seeing that the demand for day care and after-school care is fully met in ten years; it urges the extension of parental insurance schemes and active work to influence the "negative attitude of employers" toward fathers who take child-care leaves. The report endorses legislation to protect the interests of partners who live together without formal marriage, and asks for housing and transport planned to serve working parents. The program concludes with a list of "musts" to overcome the obstacles that prevent women from taking part in trade-union work.[8]

The TCO is equally adamant on these subjects. Moreover, the white-collar confederation "demands a job valuation that will put a premium on the human and social importance of work." A 1978 TCO factsheet makes the point that while the role of women has been thoroughly analyzed, "there is a very urgent need for similar analysis of the role of men," which "could increase the motivation of men for playing an active part in achieving equality between the sexes."[9]

The trade unions in Sweden have literally preempted feminist demands, and have put their political clout behind most of the specific legislative proposals to advance equality between women and men. The majority of the legislative goals relating to family law, taxation, social policy, day care, and education have been realized or are in the process of being realized.

This success has left the unions free to pursue the questions of equality at the workplace and in their own decision-making bodies very much at their own pace and on their own terms. There has been very little pressure from below; no confrontation with angry or impatient feminists. Indeed, LO made clear from the beginning that work for equality was to be conducted through the trade unions, the sole representatives of workers on the job. LO's position, as one observer (male) has put it, was: "No special feminist groups on the labor market; no special feminist groups in our organization or at our local working place." This attitude has been described as one-part male apprehension, one-part Swedish concern for union prerogatives, and one part traditional Social Democratic ideology, which has always subordinated women's rights to class questions.

Progress in promoting women's activity in the unions has been slow, if indeed it can be called real progress. Because of structural changes in LO and a policy of amalgamating small locals, three-quarters of all union branches disappeared between 1960 and 1975. This naturally led to a decrease in the proportion of women officials, since it is at the lowest, club level that women are active. "In 1972 feminine representation in the various agencies of the LO was lower than in 1959, the only year for which we have comparable figures," writes Qvist.[10] A 1973 LO study commented on "positions of power being given increasingly to men."[11] Not until 1979 did a woman—the chairman of the LO Council for Family Affairs—serve on the central negotiating body which negotiates the basic wage agreements with the employers' federation. Although women are now (1979) 38 percent of LO members, there is no woman on the LO Executive Board; there is no woman president of a national union, although there are seven unions in which women are a majority of members. Women average 9 percent on the executive boards of national unions, 14 percent on their central negotiating bodies, and 13 percent on their regional executives. The situation varies from union to union, of course, with some having no women in these posts and others having a relatively high percent, but in no case is their representation in proportion to their membership (see Table 6). At present LO is concentrating on one district (out of 240) where attitudes toward the equality drive are "very positive" and where it is believed that a model for recruiting women to office could be developed. "Most districts don't see the connection between equality and labor-market questions," according to a spokesperson for LO.

TCO was reorganized into districts after the LO model in 1977, after which representation of women on district executive boards dropped from 29 percent to 25 percent. While the white-collar confederation represents a membership that is currently 52 percent female, according to Margareta Carlestam, secretary of the TCO Family Policy Committee (which has a male chairman), "the typical TCO official is a man, middle aged, and in the middle of the job hierarchy." Women were 28 percent of delegates to the TCO congress in 1979 (up from 16 percent in 1973), but they are 15 percent of members of TCO's central board (down from 20 percent in 1972).

The Family Policy Committee's strategy has been first to create a network of equality delegates at the district level. These individuals are now working with varying success, holding courses and conferences and bringing pressure on the national unions to put women in office. The largest affiliate, the Union of Clerical and Technical Workers in Industry, already has 1,500 equality delegates at the local level—that is, in almost all firms. These conduct the same kind of "nagging" activity: to get more women involved, to put equality on the agenda of every meeting, to see that women are sent to the centrally organized long-term union courses.

Another affiliate, the Union of Commercial and Salaried Employees, has set itself the goal of 40 percent women in all union bodies by 1986, with 55 percent the ultimate target. Their principal tactic is to put up women for all posts where the incumbent is not running for reelection. Or if men seem reluctant to retire, they will expand the board or committee and elect women to the additional posts. By inviting alternates (usually women) to all meetings and electing a chairperson from the membership to preside over each meeting, they expect to help more women overcome their shyness about speaking out in public. This is the most detailed and specific plan yet worked out by any union.

Although the officials of both the LO and TCO family-policy bodies keep up a brave front, their frustration stemming from isolation in a sea of male power is obvious. Parity is a long way off according to TCO's Carlestam, not only because women are inexperienced, lacking in self-confidence, and not trained to work in teams, but because they do not yet get the support from their mates and families which everyone who combines a job with union activity needs. In her view, 'It's normal for a man to get that support, but it's not normal for a woman. Husbands can't accept it. They want to be the foremen for their wives and to be responsible for the economy of the family."

There appear, however, to be much more basic questions that stand in the way of a substantially greater voice for women in the trade unions, and which suggest that the trade unions are not going to be the route through which Swedish women reach equality. These are questions of economic interest and political clout. Activity in the blue-collar confederation is a direct route to political power. Branches have the right to affiliate their members as a group to the local Social Democratic Party organization, and one-third of LO members are joined to the party in this way, making up 70 percent of party membership. Skilled workers naturally dominate the union leadership, and the Metalworkers' Union, as the strongest single union in Sweden, stands at the center of union power. Korpi has shown that of Social Democratic metalworkers with elected union functions, 46 percent also hold elected positions in political organizations and 21 percent hold elected posts in local government.[12] The influential union men who see the connection between sex-role equality and the general situation of the workers in their working life is small. In the short term, sex-role equality is a footpath off the main road for the unions. The chief issue today is industrial democracy, or a bigger say for the unions in the way the economy is run.

Since World War II, LO has presented a common economic program with the Social Democratic Party, emphasizing the goal of full employment—to be achieved through greater efficiency in

industry. They have jointly put forward increasingly detailed programs for advancing the interests of workers through economic expansion. They have counted on translating higher productivity
through technological and structural change into higher wages and
better working conditions. This "bigger piece of a bigger cake"
economic philosophy has been successful up to a point; but as
noted in Chapter 1, it became apparent in the sixties that it was not
bringing about a real redistribution of wealth. Furthermore, as
Korpi observes, growth had been achieved on terms largely dictated
by the employers, with profit the motive, regardless of the socialist rationale for the theory.[13] The idea that economic growth, if
properly managed, is the source of all good, was increasingly ques-
tioned in Sweden as elsewhere. The women's movement was only
one part of the protest wave against consumer values. There was a
demand for a more humane working environment, for the protection of resources, for the participation of individuals in the decisions that affect their lives on the job. The voices opposing power
were gaining strength. Criticism that the trade-union movement
was an overcentralized monolith had to be answered.

Parties to the right of the Social Democrats as well as to the
left came forward with proposals to decentralize power and protect the environment. Higher worker turnover and absenteeism
prompted management studies of job satisfaction and the redesign
of work routines to reduce monotony. The clearest signal that
trade-union prestige was at a low point was the wave of wildcat
strikes in the winter of 1969–70.

By 1971 the blue-collar confederation had decided that industrial democracy was a goal equal in importance with better
wages and conditions. Since this demand was aimed at prerogatives
that the employers were not prepared to give up, LO abandoned
its traditional strategy of agreement through direct negotiations
with the employers and called for legislation. TCO joined in asking
for a review of labor laws with a view to increasing union power.
The Social Democratic Party gave its full support, and in the first
half of the seventies Parliament passed a series of pro-labor laws,
which among other things considerably restricted the right of employers to hire and fire and to allot work (1974), gave union safety
supervisors greater powers (1973 and 1977), and afforded shop
stewards more rights and better job protection (1974). Workers'
representatives received the right to sit on corporate boards with

access to all company information, in accord with legislation passed in 1973 and strengthened in 1976.

Potentially the most important piece of legislation took effect in 1977. The "Law on Co-determination" requires that employers approach the local union and ask for negotiations before instituting any important changes in operations or working conditions. The kinds of issues that LO and TCO are asking to have covered in the first central agreement with the employers' association (which would then be followed by more detailed contracts at the industry and local level) include participation in all personnel planning and training, job organization and supervision, the way data processing is introduced, and access to information on all finance and planning, including the right to bring in union consultants from the outside.

So far, basic agreements on co-determination have been signed with the national government covering salaried state employees, and with the Swedish State Holding Co. covering blue- and white-collar workers in state-owned plants. These incorporate the unions' major demands. The private employers' federation has dug in its heels and refused to accept the unions' proposal, offering its own watered-down version.

Exactly how all this legislation will work in practice, and whether it will be followed eventually by more direct steps toward worker ownership (such as was proposed in the now-shelved LO Meidner Plan of 1976, according to which a percentage of company profits would be paid out annually to the appropriate unions in the form of shares) is not the issue here. The point is that all the new agreements open up a considerable new area of union activity at every level, calling for experience and specialized training in decision making.

A new corps of knowledgeable union members must be created who are also potential future political leaders. One in every 25 union members will have to receive up to 40 hours of technical training in occupational safety. Negotiators, members of economic committees, worker board members, all have to acquire some basic knowledge of economic analysis, planning, investment and finance. "Never before have shop stewards been given such concentrated schooling to prepare them for boardroom negotiations on work organization, personnel policy, investments, marketing and other matters previously regarded as management rights," wrote Birger Viklund, a secretary of the Swedish Metalworkers' Union and former labor attaché in Washington, in 1977. "Undoubtedly," he added, "the trainees came from a group of local shop stewards and union officials who were relatively well qualified even before-hand."[14] Viklund estimates that 50,000 union members now need to be trained every year for union appointments of one kind or another.

Obviously the people who have already filled responsible trade-union functions of some kind are predominantly male. Even assuming the greatest good will toward the goal of sex-role equality, any pressure directed at persuading men to take more time off to be with their families will be countered by pressure to undertake intensive trade-union education. The unions are not prepared to argue with the findings of a government Advisory Committee on Working Hours, which reported in 1978 that a 2.5-hour reduction in the work week would rule out any substantial growth in GNP and thus any increase in wages. LO claims that its members lost purchasing power equivalent to one month's wages between 1976 and 1979. They translated this claim into action in the big strike-and-lockout confrontation of May 1980, interrupting 70 years of labor peace. The outcome was pay increases averaging 7 percent. But wage issues aside, polls have shown that the majority of LO members do not rate a six-hour day as a priority demand. According to Liljeström, "A six-hour workday has been described in Sweden as a reform for women, while a strong male opinion has been for a four-day week. The whole issue has been put on the shelf for the time being."

With the present low level of women's involvement in trade-union activities, it is inevitable that union training for positions that carry power and influence will continue to go overwhelmingly to men. The structure of the labor force, and thus of union membership, makes it *a priori* impossible for women to have an important voice in the private sector, which is where the real struggle for industrial democracy now and in the future will take place. More than 40 percent of the unionized blue-collar women work for the state or the municipalities; another 40 percent are employed in privately operated services. Only 18 percent work in industry. Women are a mere 16 percent of the country's most powerful union, the Metalworkers. About half of TCO women work for private firms, but they are of course the least skilled and lowest paid of industry's white-collar workers. They are the clerical force, while men make up the supervisors and technical experts.

There is a real danger that more industrial democracy will widen the power gap between women and men simply because, in the key branches where the vital economic decisions are made, women are so poorly represented.

While one occasionally finds official optimism at the top about the future for women in union activity, one tends to meet disenchanted women at the bottom. This has been documented by a survey made in the Political Science Department of the University of Uppsala in the mid-seventies. According to these findings, there is surprisingly high consensus among LO members and the central leadership. But while at the top of the scale are 26 percent of union branches characterized by strong approval and a high degree of activity, at the other end are 30 percent of branches where the membership is passive, where there is a low degree of concensus. In the latter there are large numbers of immigrant workers and women.[15]

Women often talk about the gap between the leadership and the membership, and the way the same people remain in the same posts year after year. The lack of responsiveness is contrasted with the situation in politics, where candidates are elected by popular vote at regular intervals and where an increase in the number of women elected takes place from term to term. "The public has access to elections, but I can't influence anything in my trade union," said a blue-collar woman. "No one can force them to put a woman on the ballot. It's a very elaborate system." There is no coalition of labor-union women in Sweden. "If the women really got together and cooperated, maybe they could do something. It would mean a fight from the bottom, though, and most of the women are low income, badly educated, and busy with their families." "You can choose your political party, but you are born into a trade union!" commented one TCO member.

Regarding what women can expect from their unions in the way of help in obtaining job equality, the labor historian Gunnar Qvist, who makes no secret of his sympathies for the disgruntled women, views the prospects with considerable reserve. It will take ten years, he thinks, to see any results from the 1977 agreements on equality signed by the union confederations with SAF, the employers' body: "The purpose of these agreements was to stop legislation on a federal scale." While the unions were ready to ask for assistance from legislators on the question of power sharing, they could not countenance the idea of legislation that would require affirmative action and provide the machinery for enforcing it, according to Qvist, who explains:

> The law on equality is seen as a threat to the unions' power. It makes it possible, in theory at least, to act in opposition to the unions. The unions are used to having the last say, and once a union has accepted a rule the member has no opportunity to oppose it.

He sees a bigger conflict of interest between the male unions and their female members than between the unions and the employers. "Employers and unions have the same interest in a bigger cake. The unions would like to share power with the employers. Otherwise they view a world run pretty much along the same lines."

On this last point, a relevant question for the eighties has been raised by Gunhild Kyle, a teacher and a speaker and writer on feminist issues: "If the companies go on working in the same way, what does it matter who runs them?"

Notes

1. Werner Thönnessen, *The Emancipation of Women; The Rise and Decline of the Women's Movement in German Social Democracy 1863-1933* (London: Pluto Press, 1973).

2. Dorothea Gaudart and Rose Marie Greve, "International Symposium on Women and Industrial Relations: Analysis of the Discussions," in *Women and Industrial Relations*, Research Series No. 54 (Geneva: International Institute for Labor Studies, 1980), p. 2.

3. Alice Cook, "Women in Trade Unions," in *Women and Industrial Relations*, Research Series No. 56 (Geneva: International Institute for Labor Studies, 1980), p. 13.

4. Thönnessen, *Emancipation of Women*, pp. 40, 47.

5. Gunnar Qvist, "The Landsorganisationen (LO) in Sweden and Women in the Labor Market (1898-1973)," *International Journal of Sociology* 5, no. 4 (1975-76): 126.

6. Ibid., pp. 130-32.

7. May-Britt Carlsson, "Sweden: Women and the Labour Market," photocopy (Stockholm, n.d.), p. 5.

8. *The Trade Union Movement and the Family Policy: Report pre-*

sented to the 1976 Congress of the Swedish Trade Union Confederation—Summary (Stockholm: LO, 1977).

9. "TCO's View of Family Policy and Equal Opportunities," TCO factsheet, Stockholm, May 15, 1978.

10. Qvist, "The Landsorganisationen," p. 136.

11. Elisabet Sandberg, *Equality is the Goal* (Stockholm: The Swedish Institute, 1975), p. 78.

12. Walter Korpi, *The Working Class in Welfare Capitalism* (London: Routledge & Kegan Paul, 1978), p. 302.

13. Ibid., p. 108.

14. Birger Viklund, "Education for Industrial Democracy," *Current Sweden* 152 (1977): 1,8.

15. Leif Lewin, "Union Democracy," *Current Sweden* 172 (1977): 5.

CHAPTER 4

The Family as Individuals

"Discussion of fathering is becoming fashionable. . . . Men are being urged to participate in the lives of their children, from conception on. . . ."

Robert A. Fein, "Research on Fathering"
Journal of Social Issues, No. 1., 1978

The conventional division of roles in the home, which in turn has justified male domination of life outside its four walls, has received its most important support from the persistent and pervasive conviction that a small child needs constant contact with its mother, and that a mother is the "natural" caretaker of her offspring at least until they are old enough to go to school. The idea of a mother's irreplaceability has continued to enjoy the status of conventional wisdom even though the number of mothers of preschool children employed outside the home has been growing steadily in all the industrialized countries for the past two decades. The Swedish "parental insurance," which pays benefits to any parent who takes leave from a job to stay home with a new baby, is the most important blow to this myth since the Soviet Union began to establish day nurseries for the infants of working mothers in the 1930s, or since the Israeli Kibbutzim proved that children raised from birth in a stable collective could grow up successfully with a very limited amount of care from their natural parents. The paid parental leave has taken the argument one step further, and legally established the competence of fathers not only to change diapers and warm bottles but to cuddle babies, whisper to them, and perhaps be the ones to see the first real smile—and on weekdays as well as Sundays.

So far the advantage of the Swedish parental leave over the more conventional maternity leave has been largely symbolic. The possibility of a more equal division of tasks is no longer in the future. It is there, creating waves on the other side of the Baltic Sea. A standard feature story for journalists from the rest of Europe in the slow summer season explores the revelations, both emotional and intellectual, that Lars (or Kurt or Bengt) experiences staying home all day with his three-year-old son and six-month-old daughter while his wife is away at work. In 1974, the first year parental leave was available, reporters noted that 2 percent of fathers took advantage of their opportunity. In 1976 it was 7 percent, in 1979 about 12 percent stayed home with the baby for six weeks to two months. The remainder of the leave (which now totals twelve months) was taken by the mother. The journalists always dutifully point out that Lars is an architect (or works in the civil service), while his wife is an economist (or a teacher). So far the leave does appeal primarily to professionals and is more easily accepted by employers in the public sector than by blue-collar workers and their employers in private enterprise. In 1978 it became illegal for an employer to refuse leave, but there are ways of making clear that an extended absence may interfere with upward mobility. On the other hand, the concentration of the first courageous fathers in government departments and social organizations has created mutual support groups which may be of importance in encouraging the trend.

Another Swedish step that may eventually make childcare seem more natural to fathers provides for voluntary parental training during paid working hours. Fathers as well as mothers may now attend ten hours of instruction before their baby is born and another ten hours afterward. Furthermore, fathers are invited to the maternity hospital after the birth for a day of instruction, during which they have an opportunity to handle and care for their own child.

In Great Britain and the United States the idea of consciously using family policy to create specific attitudes toward parental roles would have a hard time gaining a hearing. Indeed, the idea of family policy as such is not generally accepted, although numerous policies exist that affect the situation of families either directly or indirectly. Of Great Britain, Peter Moss has written: "Not only is there no such policy in this country, but the very idea of Family

Policy is not yet a familiar concept in the English speaking world."[1] In the "reluctant countries," among which Kamerman and Kahn also classify the United States, Canada, and Israel, family life is "a vital intimate sanctuary" governed by a variety of value systems on whose relative virtues the government is not entitled to pass judgement.[2]

On the European continent, however, both Western and Eastern countries (although with a considerable time lag in the case of the latter) have accepted a concept of family policy which, as Moss defines it, is "concerned with all families, and not just minority groups labeled 'deprived' or 'disadvantaged,' and is applied across a wide range of fields to any facet of society which may affect the family and is amenable to intervention."[3] They use a combination of medical and social insurance, paid maternity leave, maternity grants, family allowances, day care, and other benefits to achieve more or less openly stated aims. France and most of the East European countries follow policies aimed at income maintenance and at encouraging births. Austria is primarily concerned with protecting the interests of children, regardless of family status. Denmark stresses the goal of child development, but is also concerned with the equalization of income differentials caused by the presence or absence of children in a family. Norway has begun to include among its aims measures to enable women to work, as a way of *strengthening* the family.[4]

In all these countries family policy works to maintain the traditional division of gender roles by taking no, or—as in the case of Norway and Denmark—still ambiguous, steps to break it down. According to a Danish authority, "Our relatively well-developed policy of day care facilities favors those families . . . in which the mother takes a job outside the home," but the public subsidization of day care "does not justify a conclusion that it is the stated aim of Denmark's family policy to have children brought up in public institutions and mothers employed outside the home."[5] Sweden is so far the only country whose family policy is intended to transform the living pattern "from a family with specialized roles for the woman and the man to a family with shared roles."[6] It is doing so by designing policies that encourage the economic independence of every adult. The target is the individual, and the extent to which her or his position is defined by sex, marital status, parenthood, or age is minimized. Sweden has gone a long way toward establishing a social policy directed toward women (and men and children) as people rather than as units in a family who are not necessarily affected in the same way by policies designed to benefit the family as a whole. This individuation is applied to varying degrees in family law, in social security, in taxation, and in children's benefits. Two questions immediately spring to mind: How consistently can this aim be carried out? How far can such a policy contribute to equality between women and men?

It has been officially accepted in Sweden that the nuclear family is no longer the only conceivable form of cohabitation or social institution for raising children, and that legal protection must be extended to people who have chosen other life styles. The equality of partners in marriage had already been established by the Marriage Code of 1920, which placed responsibilities for mutual support on man and wife (homemaking being given equal weight with earned income) and made each legally independent and entitled to an equal share in joint property. When in 1969 the Minister of Justice instructed the Family Law Reform Commission, whose job it was to advance proposals for bringing the law up to date, he declared:

> In my opinion a new law ought to be neutral as far as possible in relation to different forms of cohabitation and different ethical beliefs. Marriage has and should have a central place in family law, but efforts should be made to ensure that legislation in this field does not contain any provisions which create unnecessary difficulties or disadvantages for those who have children and settle down without getting married.[7]

He also observed that

> there is no reason to abstain from using marriage and family legislation as one of several instruments in reform toward a society where every adult individual can take responsibility for himself without being economically dependent on relatives and where equality between men and women is a reality.[8]

Taking these instructions seriously, the commission made recommendations that resulted in a first-stage reform of the marriage and divorce laws in 1973. This brought the situation of married and "cohabiting" couples closer together, but it did not wipe out all differences between them. The innovative aspect of the law was its strengthening of the father's right to his child, both in and out of marriage.

The concept of "illegitimacy" lost its legal validity in Sweden in 1917, and since that year every child has had a legal father who has been required to contribute toward its maintenance. According to Birgitta Linnér, for many years a family counselor in Stockholm, court suits to establish paternity are relatively rare; the father voluntarily acknowledges his child in more than 90 percent of cases.[9] If the mother is unable to collect the maintenance due the child from the father, a minimum welfare grant is advanced to her by the state while legal proceedings are under way. Since 1970 any child born out of wedlock has had the same rights of inheritance as one born to married parents, and the same right to its father's name. Until recently, however, custody of the child of unmarried parents was automatically awarded to the mother.

The 1973 family law provides that custody of children of unmarried parents who part company should be decided according to the same rules as those governing custody in the case of divorce; that is, if the parents cannot agree, the court decides custody according to the best interests of the child. The right of the unmarried parent who does not obtain custody is protected in the same way as that of a divorced parent. Since 1977 it has been possible for unmarried parents to agree to share the legal custody of their child just as married parents do, and for both categories of parents to agree to share custody in the event that their relationship is broken off.

Another respect in which the new law treats cohabiting couples like married couples is in the assignment of the joint dwelling in case of separation. Where the couple has children, the right to the dwelling may be given to the partner whose need is greatest, provided they are not living on the private property of one of the partners.

Even after these changes, however, there still remained important differences between the status of married and unmarried partners in the eyes of the law. The Family Law Reform Commission argued that it was not possible for family law to take an entirely neutral position, and made the point that certain distinctive legal effects must stem from a legal contract between two people. In the summary of its findings, the commission said that full application of the neutrality principle, "by consistently creating the same rule for unmarried as for married cohabitants would deprive marriage of its material content as a legal institution. It would also be inconsistent with the statement in the terms of reference that marriage should have a central position in family legislation also in the future." The commission also pointed to the difficulty of defining legally a state of cohabitation to which the same rules should apply as to marriage. Moreover, suppose such a couple did not *want* to be legally defined? The effect of neutrality might run counter to the wishes of the cohabitants "if they have remained unmarried simply for the purpose of avoiding a legal regulation of their relationship."[10]

In keeping with this argument, the 1973 law does not place the mutual obligation to support each other on cohabiting unmarried couples as does the law governing marriage. Similarly, the court cannot ask one partner to pay maintenance to the other in case of separation. Since alimony is now rarely awarded in divorce, and if so, then only for a transitional period, this difference is not of major importance. More troublesome is the question of joint property in case unmarried partners split up. This problem was to be dealt with in the second stage of family law reform, which was still not complete in the spring of 1980, although the commission's proposals were expected in the course of the year. The long period of gestation can be explained by the controversial nature of some of the demands the commission was asked to consider.

Gabriel Romanus, a Liberal Party MP and member of the Family Law Reform Commission who has also served as the Minister for Social Affairs, sums up the reformers' views this way:

> We don't aim to do away with all the differences—otherwise we might as well abolish marriage, and we're not up to that. However, it's one of the tasks of the state to protect the weaker party in any relationship, so the state can't stay out of it entirely. With a couple it's usually the woman who is in the weak position. They have been living together for a number of years, she has been buying the food, he has bought the car and the TV set. It ends up with her owning nothing and he owns everything. That's not very fair.

The commission's original idea was to distinguish between marriages and nonmarriages by making all property acquired by married couples subject to equal division on divorce unless otherwise agreed, whereas for partners who did not marry only certain articles acquired for common use would be covered, such as a house or furnishings. The problem was how this would apply to other relationships—for example, to two students living together or to a homosexual partnership. Young people who only wanted to share an apartment might end up finding that one owned half the other's stereo.

The solution the commission is proposing is that in "a marriage-like relationship" it will be assumed that the rules governing common property apply unless otherwise agreed. In other relationships the reverse will be true: property will remain individual unless those involved specify that they want possessions acquired for their common use to be owned in common. According to Romanus, "The more militant homosexuals who have been pressing for legal recognition of homosexual marriage will not be satisfied, but I think they will agree that it is a step forward toward equal status."

Certainly the task of framing a law to protect the interests of unmarried couples would never have been presented to parliament in terms of observing "neutrality" toward different forms of cohabitation if the respectability of unmarried relationships had not already been widely accepted. Twenty years ago Sweden was idealized by males from other countries as a paradise of easy sex, usually to their ultimate disillusionment. Now in the Contraceptive Age it is easier for outsiders to hear what the Swedes have been saying about themselves all along: permissiveness is not the same thing as promiscuity. When Alva Myrdal wrote in 1941 that "the marriage ceremony is less valued and the absence of it less of a taboo in Sweden than in most other countries," she was not describing a uniquely lax regard for conventional morality.[11] She was summing up the consequences of several centuries of socioeconomic circumstances that contributed to a low marriage rate and relative tolerance concerning children born out of wedlock.

When, as in Sweden at the start of the twentieth century, marriage customs were still strongly influenced by the importance of land as property, wealthy landowners obviously valued the marriage contract and the principle of legitimacy as a way of keeping property in the family. The church lent its moral support to their interests. Yet, in spite of the strong emphasis on the sanctity of marriage and severe punishment of adultery (defined to include sexual relations between unmarried people), the marriate rate decreased during the entire period between 1750 and 1900. Most of the population consisted of small and middle farmers; where the land was already divided it was important not to subdivide it further, so that marriage was postponed and many people never married at all. To complement this situation, in sparsely settled northern Sweden, where land was plentiful and society relatively egalitarian, premarital sexual relations were an institutionalized form of courtship. There was nothing casual about such a relationship; it was regarded as a binding commitment. Yet it was not unusual for the actual wedding ceremony to take place after one or more children had been born. Loose relationships, on the other hand, were strongly condemned by the community and a resulting illegitimate child was a disgrace; many such mothers never found a husband.

The increase in the landless poor between 1830 and 1850 and the wave of emigration in the following decades led to a surplus of women, a decreasing frequency of marriage, and a steady rise in illegitimacy. In the last decade of the century more than 10 percent of all children were born out of wedlock. Babies were frequently abandoned by their mothers, living in poverty and faced with social humiliation; infanticide was not uncommon. The burden that unmarried mothers represented for society, rather than some unexplained Swedish radicalism, led to the abolition of the legal stigma of illegitimacy in 1917 and explains why the children of unwed mothers acquired some legal rights before World War I.[12]

Myrdal makes the interesting point that the traditional lax village attitude toward sexual relations between young people persisted so long that it ultimately coincided with the development of modern patterns attributable to the secularization of the Swedish people, the growth of socialist sentiments, and the rise of ideas concerning women's emancipation and free love in the late nineteenth century.[13] Among the most prominent advocates of free sexual relations between women and men, unfettered by laws and conventions, was Ellen Key, a Swedish writer and educator who lectured at the Workers' Institute in Stockholm from 1870 to 1890. She also toured the European continent, where her writings, published in translation, had made her famous. One of those she influenced was Alexandra Kollontai, a dedicated advocate of women's rights in Russia who later attempted vainly to propagate new ideas of sexual morality during the first years of the Soviet government.[14]

It is hardly surprising that a trend whose continuity can be traced through 200 years of Swedish social history should leave its mark on the present. In the 1960s, 20 percent of Swedish adults had never married, compared to 10 percent in the United States. The number of weddings fell by 35 percent between 1966 and 1971, and in the latter year only 57 percent of all Swedish women aged 15 to 44 were married, compared to 68 percent in England and Wales. As far as births outside wedlock are concerned, Sweden has advanced from third place in Europe in 1960, with 13.3 per 100 live births, to overwhelming ascendancy, with nearly one-third of all children born to unmarried parents in 1975 (compared to 9.7 percent in England and Wales), and 35 percent in 1979.

While marriages between young people have declined, the divorce rate has risen; this is in contrast to the situation in some other European countries where an increase in divorce parallels a trend toward early marriage. The Swedes like to stress that this has not affected the value placed on fidelity as long as a relationship lasts. According to the "Swedish Kinsey Report" compiled in 1969, 87 percent of men and 92 percent of women considered faithfulness in marriage essential. Today two-thirds of unmarried parents continue to live together after their child is born, and half of all couples whose child is born outside matrimony later legalize their relationship. Nevertheless, it appears that Sweden is moving faster than most other advanced industrialized countries toward a society of cohabiting individuals, temporary families, and single individuals with or without children. By 1976 one out of every two marriages ended in divorce, and the proportion of one-parent families had reached two in every nine—double the figure for Great Britain. "Family" policy, although its aim at present is to encourage the creation of a "symmetrical" family in which responsibilities are shared equally, must be flexible enough to protect society's weaker individuals in all these emerging situations—that is, children particularly, but as long as real sex-role equality does not exist, women as well.

Social security is an area in which many Swedish measures

have from the beginning focused on the individual rather than the family; but this is more the consequence of the original effort to protect nonearners in general than of considerations of sex-role equality. Everyone who lives in Sweden is covered by compulsory health insurance, paid for by employers' contributions and tax-financed state grants. Each person is individually insured, regardless of marital status, sex, or employment. Describing the Swedish approach, Grönwall and Lindberg point out that the system in many European countries whereby family members who are not gainfully employed derive the right to care from the insurance of an employed member has no counterpart in Sweden.[15] Hospital care is completely free, and for all dependent children and all persons over 65 this is true of visits to the doctor or dentist as well. Others pay a low fixed fee. Employed persons receive benefits amounting to 90 percent of pay during illness. A person with no earned income can, however, obtain a minimum sickness benefit if she or he is insured as a homemaker.

A basic old-age pension is paid to everyone over 65, regardless of previous employment, at uniform rates (in 1977, the equivalent of $2,335 annually); it is financed by a payroll tax and state grants. All persons who have been employed are also entitled to an income-related supplementary pension, which is entirely financed by the employers. Pensioners who are entitled to the basic pension only or who receive a very small supplementary pension are paid a further pension supplement. To this a wife's supplement and a municipal housing allowance may be added, subject to a means test.

Because older women who have never worked outside the home are at an obvious disadvantage, widows are still paid a supplementary pension on the basis of their husband's supplementary pension rights, but this provision, which contradicts the goal of making benefits independent of family status, will eventually be phased out. It is in fact impossible to be wholly consistent in this transition period. For example, consideration is being given to the idea of allotting one-half of a husband's social-security credits to his wife in cases where an older woman with poor pension expectations is divorced (and thus has lost not only her share in her husband's income but her rights to a widow's pension as well). The idea of granting supplementary pension benefits in recognition of work in the home has been considered by parliament but rejected on the grounds that homemakers are already entitled to the basic pension and this, together with parental insurance benefits, provides coverage for the periods when an adult is normally at home without offering an inducement to full-time homemaking. The situation of women (or men) who must stay home with a dependent child or adult for whom no other care is available is to be solved by social-security benefits related specifically to care for another person.

The present old-age pension scheme provides a certain incentive for women to work because of the low eligibility requirements for the supplementary pension: three years employment amounting to at least 16 hours a week is all that is needed to qualify for minimum benefits. The number of women who have no credits toward a pension supplement is shrinking. By 1975, three-quarters of all women aged 40—50 were earning credits, and by 1985 the vast majority of all women will be covered, although at a lower level than men. In 1976 women's pensions averaged only one-half of men's, and this situation is likely to improve only very slowly.[16]

The introduction of unemployment benefits for persons not eligible for unemployment insurance (because they have not been employed, in labor-market training, or on parental leave for five months out of the last twelve) is also, in practice, of special benefit to housewives entering the labor market, whether or not they have ever worked outside the home before. As long as they are registered as seeking work, they can draw cash assistance for up to 150 days. Like regular unemployment benefits, this income is taxable and therefore carries supplementary pension rights.

Individual taxation, introduced in 1971, makes it more profitable for a wife to work even at a part-time job than for her husband to take on a few extra hours. Some authors consider the change in the tax law to be the reform that has done the most to promote equality between the sexes.[17] Some elements of cotaxation remain, however: income from capital is cotaxed, and there is a small deduction allowed for a dependent spouse. This is another interim measure intended to protect those families in which the wife, due to her age, is unlikely to go out and look for a job. There is only a small income-tax deduction for dependent children; instead, parents are reimbursed through the uniform allowance paid for all children and the benefits in kind that children receive— free education, free school books, lunches, and transport to school, free medical and dental care, and subsidized day care. A family's

number of children in relation to income determines its eligibility
for a housing allowance, currently paid to about half of all complete families with children and 90 percent of one-parent families.
Women, particularly, have gained a degree of economic security from all these measures that is not dependent on family status
or employment. Inequalities between men and women are per-
petuated, nevertheless, insofar as benefits above the minimum are
income-related. Here a woman is almost automatically in a worse
position than a man because of her lower earnings and shorter
working experience. One illustration will suffice to show how difficult it is to combine in social policy the goals of protecting the
weak, treating all individuals equally, encouraging all adults to be
self-supporting, and remaining neutral with regard to forms of cohabitation. Single parents (single mothers in more than 90 percent
of cases) are usually the heads of low-income families, and are
therefore entitled to favorable tax deductions and a rent allowance, as well as child-support payments from the other parent (or
an advance payment by the state) and priority in obtaining a day-
care place. Since the rent allowance is income-related it is of
course suspended if a companion of either sex with an income
moves in. The temptation not to report this change in status is
great, but if it comes to the attention of the local authorities resti-
tution has to be made for the back rent (although the day-care
place is never taken away). The situation is not as conflict-ridden
as it is in countries where a single parent receives a special allowance that can be canceled if that parent (usually a woman) forms
a new alliance. Still, it provokes similar charges of spying on people's private lives and penalizing the unmarried woman for her sex
life. Social policy in this case has removed the stigma of the "welfare mother" by treating the woman as the head of a low-income
family. She can combine the benefits to which she is entitled with
gainful work in whatever way suits her particular situation. Social
policy is powerless, however, to affect the reality that the main
reason such a family is "low-income" is that it is headed by a
woman, and that her chances of escaping from this economic category are minimal unless she finds another partner. At present
about 20 percent of all families with children under 18 are in this
position.[18]

Measures that are intended to promote a more equal distribution of income sometimes act to counter a more equal division of

sex roles. The progressive tax rate combined with the income-tested housing allowance can make it more profitable for a wife to choose part-time instead of full-time employment, lest she increase the family income to a point where the housing allowance will be lost while income tax rises. Or, a couple whose income is above the ceiling for a rent allowance may find it more economical to buy a house in the suburbs, since interest payments on a mortgage can be deducted from taxes. This move in turn may make it more difficult for the wife to work full time or may limit her job opportunities.

Yet another reason why Swedish social policy does not proceed along a straight highway clearly bound for sex-role equality is that every step is inevitably a compromise between the Social Democratic and Communist parties on the left, the Center and Conservative parties on the right, and the Liberals in the middle.

Although all the parties are committed to equality, and their differences on the ultimate goals of family policy seem comparatively minor when one considers the situation in many other countries, there are distinctly partisan differences when it comes to specific policy measures. In line with the demands of Social Democratic women, that party has given priority to day care over other forms of support to parents of small children, and in addition has been pressing for recognition of the principle that any extension of parental leave should incorporate a condition that the father use half the time (except in the case of single-parent families). The Center and Conservative parties, on their side, have been pushing for years for a childcare allowance to be paid at a flat rate to whichever parent stays home with a child after the expiration of parental leave.

The argument is between those who do not want to see any reforms that will discourage women from working or make it more advantageous for mothers rather than fathers to stay at home, and those who contend that the present system of state expenditures is unfair to those who choose to take the burden of childcare on themselves or who are not lucky enough to get a scarce day-care place. While few people today would have the temerity to argue that homemaking is women's natural role, the Conservative Party in particular maintains that nothing can replace the home as an environment for bringing up children. It speaks for those who believe that basic family values are being overturned and that the emphasis on day care and returning mothers to work denigrates the contribution of the homemaker while financially penalizing those who do not take advantage of subsidized day care. They oppose making any leave contingent upon the father's sharing it. While the Liberal Party itself favors a stress on day care, it supports the parties to its right on "the right to choose." The Social Democrats argue strongly that the introduction of a childcare allowance in the form of a flat sum will inevitably be taken by the mother, which in practice will perpetuate women's "conditional liberation" and effectively relax pressure on local governments to build more day-care centers.[19]

When the parental leave was extended from seven to nine months, under a Center-led coalition government, the Social Democrats, Liberals, and Communists banded together to win full insurance benefits for the additional two months. The Social Democrats did not succeed, however, in convincing parliament to require that the father take at least half of the additional time. The Conservative and Center parties made some progress toward a childcare allowance by achieving for parents the legal right to stay home until their child is 18 months old, the second nine months without compensation. The coalition government elected in 1979 succeeded in 1980 in extending the paid parental leave to 12 months, but with the last three months paid at a low, flat benefit rate. Its aim is to extend parental insurance to 18 months "at the rate economic resources permit."

The gradual encroachment of nonpaid and poorly paid leaves as an alternative to day care alarms women who are militant on the question of sex-role equality. Both the Social Democratic Women and the TCO Family Policy Committee favor the extension of the parental insurance to 12 months or even longer, but not without some provision governing the division of time between parents. "Every family should have time in the bank for a critical period," according to Lisa Mattson, head of the Social Democratic women's organization, "but we should use this instrument to get more division of responsibility in the home. The second six months should be divided. You can't just wait for change. You must change attitudes. If fathers were *required* to take part of the leave, there would be no question about employers discouraging them."

Margareta Carlestam, secretary of the TCO Family Committee,

regards the present government's policy of extending the leave without any such requirement as tragic. "It will be impossible in the future to take it back and say, 'Now you've got to divide it or lose it.' If it becomes possible to pay for it at the same rate as the first nine months then we *must* have some kind of quota attached to it."

Carlestam also regrets the introduction of another new option, effective since 1979, enabling parents of children under eight to reduce their workday to six hours with a commensurate loss of pay; she would oppose this even if there were no pay reduction. The objections of trade-union and other women to this selective measure are not clear at first glance. The right of parents of small children to a six-hour day should make it legal to reduce almost any job to six hours and thereby upgrade part-time work, at least theoretically. It also offers the possibility of shortening the time the smallest children spend in the day nursery, as recommended by the Family Aid Commission headed by a former Social Democratic Minister for Family Affairs, Camilla Odhnoff. The argument of the blue-collar unions that most of their members are not in a position to reduce their hours individually has been met, in principle at least, by a provision making it illegal for the employer to refuse. But the unions argue that a piecemeal dismantling of the eight-hour day will cause discrimination against young parents; while the Social Democratic women, particularly, believe that the option will be taken up primarily by women, and that giving priority to parents puts the six-hour day for everyone even more firmly on the back burner.

With the reduced workday option as with other measures taken in Sweden, new ground is being broken, the side-effects are difficult to predict, and the value of the tradeoffs is still unclear. Whatever the built-in contradictions, Swedish social policy has gone a fair way toward creating a framework in which roles can be shared and flexible arrangements can be made to suit different life situations. The extent to which people are actually able to make use of the possibilities for equality depends on factors outside the province of social policy makers, primarily in the labor market. Measures to advance sex-role equality obviously move faster in the field of social policy, because they are decided in the public sector and are an extension of welfare-state philosophy, while concessions to women on the labor market must be wrested from employers oriented toward productivity and profits, and from the unions. One factor pushing family policy forward is the simple fact that policy makers have had to take cognizance of the new realities of life represented by today's young families and nonfamilies, who are themselves the product of the sex-role equality debate, the women's movement, the radical sixties, and the current debate on the environment and resources. Vocal young people can make their views felt more successfully in the area of social policy, where, as teachers, social workers, journalists, sociologists, they are personally among the movers as well as the targets, than in the sphere of production, where they are at the bottom of the heap.

The cumulative effect of family policy is felt in the private sector of the economy only after a time lag. Initially some equality measures helped employers to meet their need for workers, by freeing women to take jobs. But in the long run, the advantages of an equality policy are questionable from the employers' point of view. The sum total of Swedish cash transfers and benefits encouraging a more equal division of roles between women and men effectively decreases dependence on wages and in so doing undermines incentives to work, or at least to work harder than is consistent with other responsibilities and interests. That the nonincome-related benefits of the welfare states conflict with industry's desire for a highly motivated workforce is not news, but this is only beginning to be analyzed as a specific dilemma in the drive for women's equality. Sociologists have expressed doubts that government policy can effect basic changes in the family that run counter to the needs of an industrial system like the Swedish, based on competitiveness and a high rate of expansion. Even if it is not the overt intention, industrial practices are more likely to modify sex-role equality in the family than is family policy to influence policies in industry.

One can imagine that if an equal division of the parental leave were to be written into the parental insurance law as a condition of eligibility, it could lead to a society of men whose energies were divided between their jobs and their children, and of women who identified with their work outside the home instead of concentrating on keeping their men in shape and preparing their children for the work force. This androgynous vision is not the generally accepted model in Sweden, however. Industry is not preparing now for a labor force of part-time workers of both sexes with loyalties to job and home in equal measure. In the words of one manager:

> Ideally, we want a worker who is 32 years old, Swedish born, with children, and lives close enough to the factory to ride a bicycle over here. If you know him, send him over.

Since this ideal worker is increasingly hard to find, Göteborg's Volvo plant—whose personnel director made the above statement in the spring of 1980—is solving the problems of high labor costs, absenteeism, and "blue-collar blues" not by redesigning jobs (as Volvo did in the 1970s); rather, it has become the European leader in the introduction of industrial robots.[20] Robotization is advancing much faster than attempts to understand what it will mean for equality, as opposed to what it could mean.

Another example is the tendency toward increased shift work throughout Western Europe (due partly to shorter working hours), although it is generally recognized as detrimental to health. In the Swedish metal industry the percent of employees working shifts rose from 13 percent in 1958 to 21 percent in 1972. Shift work in the services is also growing. Fathers who don't find shift work compatible with childcare and homemaking will probably limit their participation at home; mothers will reduce their hours or look for other work.

Under circumstances where "business as usual" prevails in the sphere of production, the moral incentives arising from the equality drive are found to make limited inroads against constraints that operate to preserve the conventional division of labor in the family. As has been seen, since 1976 there have been strong pressures for childcare arrangements that in practice would continue to place most of the responsibility on the mother. According to a 1976 study on Swedes at work by the Swedish Central Bureau of Statistics, in families where husband and wife were both employed *full time*:

  67 percent of women did all or practically all the cooking;
  50 percent did all or practically all the washing up;
  80 percent did all the laundry;
  53 percent did all or practically all the shopping;
  55 percent did all the cleaning.[21]

As for the time spent by Swedish men who did "some" of the cleaning, shopping, cooking, etc., a sample survey of 7,000 women made by the Committee on Equality in 1978 revealed that overall, including families where women were not employed full time, men spent less than half as much time as women in daily routine household tasks. "Are you pretending you are Mother?" asked one Swedish three-and-a-half-year old when she saw her father vacuuming.

A relatively advanced Swedish family policy contributes to changing both women's roles and their expectations. It encourages them not to put up with the *status quo* by offering them support as independent individuals; as a result, their threshold of disillusionment is lowered. The demands of the economy act as a brake that keeps men functioning as they have in the past, and so far only a small percent of men appear to be actively interested in changing this state of affairs. A symmetrical family remains the objective, but an increasing number of partnerships founder on the fact that the two individuals concerned are tuned to two different sets of realities. In most cases of divorce or separation, and especially where there are children, the woman exchanges her position as the weaker partner for membership in a social group that, despite all the protective measures social policy offers to the "unattached" woman, is still one of society's weakest.

Notes

1. Peter Moss, "Day Care and Family Policy" (photocopy), Thomas Coram Research Unit, London, April 1977, p. 1.
2. Hilary Land and Roy Parker, "United Kingdom," in Sheila B. Kamerman and Alfred J. Kahn, eds., *Family Policy: Government and Families in Fourteen Countries* (New York: Columbia University Press, 1978), p. 332.
3. Moss, "Day Care and Family Policy," p. 1.
4. See the relevant country chapters in the above-mentioned collection edited by Kamerman and Kahn. Pronatal family policies in Eastern Europe are discussed in Hilda Scott, "Women in Eastern Europe," in Jean Lipman-Blumen and Jessie Bernard, eds., *Sex Roles and Social Policy* (London and Beverly Hills: Sage Publications, 1979), pp. 177-98.
5. Jacob Vedel-Petersen, "Denmark," in Kamerman and Kahn, eds., *Family Policy*, p. 304.
6. R. Liljeström, "Sweden," in ibid., p. 29.
7. Birgitta Alexandersson, "The 1973 Family Law Reform," *Current Sweden* 8 (1973): 2.

8. Birgitta Linnér, *Sex and Society in Sweden* (New York: Harper Colophon, 1972), p. 130.

9. Birgitta Linnér, "No Illegitimate Children in Sweden," *Current Sweden* 157 (1977): 3; see also Linnér, *Society and Sex in Sweden* (Stockholm: The Swedish Institute, 1971), p. 27.

10. The first report of the parliamentary committee appointed to overhaul the family law is published as *Familj och Aktenskap—1* (Stockholm, 1972) (SOU—Statens offentliga utredningar [Reports on Government Public Inquiries], 1972:41), with an English summary, pp. 249-65.

11. Alva Myrdal, *Nation and Family* (Cambridge: MIT Press, 1968), p. 47.

12. Customs that condoned premarital sexual relations are discussed at length in Rita Liljeström, *A Study of Abortion in Sweden* (Stockholm: Allmänna Förlaget, 1974), chapters 1 and 2, and in Myrdal, *Nation and Family*, chapter 3.

13. Myrdal, *Nation and Family*, p. 45.

14. Cathy Porter, *Alexandra Kollontai: a Biography* (London: Virago, 1980), p. 155.

15. Lars Grönwall and Ingemar Lindberg, "Anti-Poverty Measures in Sweden: Based on Income and Cash Benefits," in *Eurosocial Reports No. 14* (Vienna: European Centre for Social Training and Research, 1979), p. 72.

16. Christina Jonung, *Women and Social Security: The Case of Sweden* (Lund: National Economic Institute of Lund University, 1978), pp. 55-56.

17. Annika Baude, "Public Policy and Changing Family Patterns in Sweden," in Lipman-Blumen and Bernard, eds., *Sex Roles and Social Policy*, p. 171.

18. In 1976, 23% of all Swedish families with children were headed by a single parent (widowed, divorced, unmarried or separated), and of these 92% were headed by women. See *Siffor om män och kvinnor* [Men and Women: Key Figures] (Stockholm: SAF, 1979), p. 50.

19. Their fears are not unfounded. These effects have been found in Hungary and Czechoslovakia, which introduced such childcare allowances in 1968 and 1971 respectively. See Hilda Scott, "Eastern European Women in Theory and Practice," *Womens' Studies International Quarterly* 1 (1978): 189-99.

20. Jonathan Kandell, "Robots Answer Volvo's Blue-Collar Blues," *International Herald Tribune*, March 31, 1980.

21. Bo A. Ericsson, "The Swedes and Their Work," *Current Sweden* 129 (1976): 7.

CHAPTER 5

A Morality for the Contraceptive Age

"Nothing has really changed for us. My friends are preoccupied with their bodies, how they look to their men. The older women in this neighborhood are worried about what will happen to them if their husbands leave them or die suddenly."

—A 38-year-old divorced mother of two

"I've got so much stronger, and I can't live with false premises any longer. That means you have a new sort of language. You say, 'I'm not living with lies any longer.' And when you use this sort of language you don't have so many men to choose from because they don't understand what you mean. Emotional consequences? What do you mean? Responsibility? What's that? I mean, they have no emotional contact with themselves. Men are trapped."

—A 30-year-old single woman living in a commune

"Now that I've got self-confidence I dare speak out more when I talk to him. But I'm awfully cautious because I'm afraid he'll feel threatened by my new independence. Maybe he doesn't feel the same strength in his relationship with me; in that case he's thinking wrong, but he doesn't know it. I've tried to put myself in his situation because it is harder for the man before he's got used to the new order. Perhaps it's more difficult in the working class. We're more like machine tools, the men are more tired when they come home and need more personal attention."[1]

—A young mother who recently took her first job

Living up to norms of sex-role equality, a subject on which they are bombarded from all sides, is very difficult for the generation of Swedish women over 35, especially as their own day-to-day existence continues to follow largely traditional patterns. Younger women are preoccupied with how to put their relationships with men on a footing of equality, and with developing criteria for looking at themselves as an alternative to seeing themselves through the eyes of men. They are torn between wanting to assert values of their own and wanting to please. Men who are not even aware that they have been reared by society to think of women as sex objects or appendages for their confort, are faced with new expectations that are hardly articulated; and they receive contradictory messages. All the concepts of masculinity that they have assimilated are threatened.

"Sex roles are not just a matter of men taking care of the baby and women going into technical jobs, and this makes it very difficult to talk about," in the words of Gunilla Hollander, one of the organizers of the "Sexuality and Human Relations" program at the Swedish National Board of Health and Welfare. Questions of sexuality are at the heart of sex-role equality, in the opinion of a small group of pioneers at this central government agency. Through its Health Education Committee they have been working since the early seventies to incorporate the sensitive realm of sexuality in the drive for sex-role equality. Sexuality in this context has a much wider meaning than the sex act, and is understood to stand for the sum total of values, feelings, and behavior patterns associated with the individual's consciousness of identity as a woman or a man. It includes the cultural meaning attached to sexual behavior in its social sense as well as its biological aspects.

In wanting to come to grips with this question, the Health Education Committee is at one with a segment of the women's movement in Sweden and elsewhere in believing that as long as society ignores the factors that shape intimate human relationships, neither labor-market programs and parental insurance nor abortion laws and contraceptives will have the transforming effect expected of them. It has been this insistence on making "sexual politics" part of the struggle for women's equality and on bringing into the open the deeply buried personal conflicts nurtured in silence that, more than anything else, has aroused hostility to the modern feminist movement and created divisions within the movement itself.

In 1973 a Swedish government department was authorized to

enter this combat zone. The department's mission was not put in these terms, of course. At this time, attention centered on the new, more liberal abortion legislation, which had been in the works since 1965. The Swedish abortion rate was not sensational in comparison to other countries that had recognized social indications for abortion. In 1973 it was 16 per 1,000 women aged 15 to 44—about on the same level as Denmark and the United States, somewhat higher than England and Wales (11.5), far below Finland and the countries of Eastern Europe.[2] Yet it represented a 400 percent increase over 1965. The mere fact that a new abortion law was known to be in preparation encouraged more women to seek abortion and more doctors to interpret liberally the indication permitting them to interrupt a pregnancy when "weakness of the mother" could be "anticipated."

What alarmed Swedish authorities particularly was the increase in teenage abortions. In 1973 girls 14 to 19 years old accounted for almost one-quarter of all abortions; 42 percent of all pregnancies in women under 20 ended in legal induced abortions, compared to 33 percent in 1971. Since the average age of girls at first intercourse had dropped from 17 in the late sixties to 16 in the early seventies, a further increase in teenage abortions could be projected. Why, in the most family-planning-conscious country in the world, where sex education had been a compulsory subject in the schools since 1956, where maternal health-service clinics were expected to give contraceptive advice to the unmarried as well as the married, and where pharmacies had been obliged to carry contraceptives since 1946, were so many women resorting to abortion?

When the Health Education Committee undertook to develop a long-term program on family planning whose main purpose was to reduce the number of legal abortions, especially among the youngest women, it was the first time the government had engaged directly in this sort of education. The provision to the public of information on sexual questions had until then been the mandate of a private body, the National Association for Sex Education, which had been founded in 1933 by a friend and associate of Margaret Sanger, Elise Ottesen-Jensen, as the Swedish Planned Parenthood Association. The National Board of Health and Welfare had focused its own educational efforts on nutrition, veneral disease, and drug abuse.

In outlining its new program, the committee started from the premise that the problem at hand involved much more than family planning, and that the real connections between sexuality, birth control, and abortion had yet to be explored. They were aware that in spite of two decades of planned sexual enlightenment, the Swedes remained at heart deeply conservative in their views. While the mechanics of sex could be aired at a superficial level, the motives determining sexual behavior remained unaffected by this technical knowledge. Though Sweden had become a trail-blazer in abortion policy in the thirties (the third country after Iceland and the Soviet Union to liberalize its laws [3]), this was due to the relative backwardness of other states rather than to radicalism in Swedish attitudes toward women.

Swedish policy had evolved from a nineteenth-century starting point little different from that in the United States, England, and other countries: women convicted of attempting to get rid of an unwanted pregnancy were liable to incur prison sentences. In Sweden, as elsewhere, women were at once the key to the secret of life and the cause of man's original (and repeated) sin, and man could not afford to let her escape from his control. Describing the "punishment syndrome" of the nineteenth century, Lawrence Lader writes:

> To the puritan mind, laws against contraception and abortion were intended to punish and degrade women, and above all, to deprive them of the possiblity of enjoying sex for its own sake. By outlawing contraception and abortion, male-dominated society assumed that a woman would be terrified to indulge in sex when a pregnancy would expose her "sin" to the world. . . . [4]

When in 1938 Sweden recognized disease, malformation, and "weakness of the mother" as social indications for legal abortion to save the woman's life or health, the aims of the Population Commission and the lawmakers did not go beyond reducing the very high rate of illegal abortions. At the same time, on the insistence of the Social Democratic Women's League, they took a more courageous step toward planned parenthood and revoked the legislation prohibiting the sale and distribution of contraceptives. Pointing to the inconsistency of purpose represented by these two measures, Elise Ottesen-Jensen commented: "The beautiful principle of voluntary parenthood which the Population Commission upholds in the contraception question kicks the legs out from under itself in the abortion question."[5] The 1938 law did little to expand women's freedom. The "weakness of the mother" indication was rarely invoked, and estimated illegal abortions continued to outnumber legal ones by twenty to one. From 1938 until the seventies, Swedish policy remained the same: to reduce illegal abortions by exempting certain especially unfortunate women from the law, which avenged itself on women who "allowed themselves" to become pregnant by requiring them to carry the pregnancy to term.

Applications for abortion still had to be signed by two doctors or approved by the National Board of Health and Welfare. The way these applications were dealt with under the same law over a 30-year period provides a barometer of contemporary public opinion. During the late forties and the early fifties that opinion was decidedly conservative. Shrill charges of infanticide were harbingers of the "right to life" debate still current today in several Western countries. Some voices called for stricter punishments for women who resorted to illegal abortion. The Swedish Established Church declared that abortion was acceptable only in cases of rape, or where the mother's life was in danger.

While in 1950 more than 6,000 abortions were performed, or about 85 percent of those requested, by 1960 the number was down to less than half, with only 62 percent of applications approved. "In 1950 it was shameful to be unmarried in such a situation, and there was real risk of suicide," according to Dr. Kajsa Sandström, now in charge of the medical aspects of family planning at the National Board of Health and Welfare. "The job of the abortion social workers was to bring pressure on the girl to have the child. Young people were forced into marriage. The whole machinery of the hierarchy was very restrictive."

During the twenty-year period from 1940 to 1960 the estimated illegal abortion rate hardly changed: it hovered around 200 per 1,000 live births. Then came the Pill, the IUD, the sex-role equality campaign, the women's movement. The appointment of a new government commission in 1965 to study the situation and propose a revised law was recognition of the gap between existing legislation and public attitudes. "The whole climate changed," according to Sandström. "It was enough for a woman to say 'I don't want a child by that man.' But the doctors still had to put a diagnosis on it, and it depended on the attitude of the doctor." The number of legal abortions rose to 6,000 in 1965, to 16,000 in 1970, and 19,000 in 1971 in anticipation of changes in the law. In that year the commission brought in its report recommending abortion on demand, free under national health insurance, saying, "We acknowledge [the woman's] ability to judge for herself whether she can take the responsibility of bearing a child."[6] Then followed several more years of emotional public debate. Not until 1974 did the government consider it strategic to put the bill before parliament. By that time the number of legal abortions had reached 30,000 while the illegal rate had dropped to nearly nothing.

It became the job of the Health Education Committee to use the implementation of the new law to lay the groundwork for a sexual morality appropriate to the Contraceptive Age. Commenting on the prevailing atmosphere in which young people were coming to terms with their sexuality in 1974, the committee said:

> (The) liberalization in the '60s has been overtaken by an increasingly raw commercial exploitation of sexuality with emphasis on consumption, performance and depersonification. . . . Development in recent years presents the paradox of a society that increasingly stands up for equality between the sexes in various fields at the same time as the sexual exploitation of women becomes more and more brazen in, for instance, the mass media and advertising. The anti-human and, in the deepest sense, anti-sexual attitudes that youth encounter today in commercial messages cannot be overemphasized.[7]

As the committee saw it, teenagers had been left to contrast the ubiquitous sexually potent and passionately liberated fantasy figures of the media with their own insecurity and inadequacy. Inhibited by the conventions of their upbringing from discussing their feelings, each partner tried to live up to what he or she thought the other expected. The committee set itself the task of finding out how to provide an alternative in the form of an open atmosphere for discussion between men and women, between generations, and between counselors and those seeking advice. They christened their area of work "sexuality and human relations," to make clear that the task of motivating young people to shift from abortions to contraceptives could not be tackled apart from the general question of what it means to become part of another individual's life, and that it required altered attitudes toward the question of sexuality on the part of adults as well as better cooperation between professional groups.

There were organizational problems whose solution needed to be stimulated from the center but which ultimately had to be solved at the county and municipal level. The first of these was the wholly inadequate network of contraceptive services. The 24 county councils were given state funds to expand and pay for counseling provided by doctors, by school nurses, and by counselors in private organizations, in addition to their regular duties.

"We couldn't tell them you *must*," recalls Sandström. "In some parts of Sweden it has been very hard to get them to expand their services, so that we have to keep the information flowing to them. We collect the members of the government in each county once a year and explain why it is their responsibility to improve, so that counseling will really be available."

Also at the central level the board organized courses for the chief physicians of the health service to present to them the implications for professional roles and medical routines of the abortion law: the right of every woman to decide for herself, the increased need for counseling which the new contraceptive methods involved, the demand for help with sexual problems free of moralizing. The chief physicians' task was in turn to organize special training at the county level for all general practitioners, school nurses, welfare officers, midwives, and others in a position to give guidance.

Special information techniques had to be worked out to reach individual target groups—decision makers, teachers, parents, youth leaders, the media. Models were developed that could be used locally. Obviously the sex education being given by the schools was not reaching the right people at the right time. Young people were not capable of applying the theoretical lectures to their own bodies. Confusion resulted from the fact that while it was still the male who usually initiated a sexual relationship, the new contraceptives put the responsibility on the young woman, who was often not prepared to take it. According to the findings of the Health Education Committee it was the least secure girls with the most traditional upbringing who, once liberated from a restrictive sexual morality, were most likely to be pushed into premature sexual activity. The similarly insecure young men, who were most threatened by the new equality and most influenced by the media, were the ones who sought to prove themselves according to the stereotypes of masculinity. In the majority of teenage relationships that resulted in pregnancy, contraceptives had not been used.

The approach Sandström found most successful was to have the school nurse give a short talk to 12- and 13-year-old girls in small groups, chatting about problems that concern them in a concrete way, like menstruation, and making it clear that if they have any questions they can come to see her.

> It's mostly to present her as a person, interested and open. The result is that, when sooner or later they have problems about sexual relationships, they do come. They know they can see her about a sprained ankle or "something for my stomach" or "are my breasts big enough?" and then it's natural for her to find out what's really bothering them and perhaps make an appointment with the midwife at the community health center where they can get oral contraceptives, the IUD, or pessaries.

The school nurse makes plain that she is bound by medical secrecy and that she is not going to inform their teacher or mother, although she tries to get girls to talk to their parents themselves. School nurses are entitled to give out foam and condoms free of charge, pessaries or intra-uterine devices are fitted at counseling centers free, and pills are dispensed on prescription at the same token charge as other subsidized drugs available under health insurance.

The theatre has proved one of the most effective mediums the Health Education Committee has found to bring to the most vulnerable young people some sense that there is a difference between superficial sensuality and sex as one facet of a deep relationship with another person. Hanna Olsson, a member of the team that drew up the committee's original program, presented the problem to five independent young theatre groups and asked them if they would be interested in creating plays around the subject of sex roles and contraception. These groups played all over the country for schools and youth organizations.

> The theatre gives people a chance to involve their emotions, and this emotional identification is very important when it comes to delicate subjects like sex. They try to imagine how they would act, and perhaps come to the conclusion they would never do anything so stupid.

The first play to make the rounds, whose title translates freely as *Knocked Up or Cracked Up*, was about the relations between a 16-year-old girl and a gang of teenage boys. Eva lets herself be talked into sexual relations with one she isn't interested in when the boy she likes fails to turn up for a date. What happens when she thinks she's pregnant, and the results of the pregnancy test fall into her father's hands provides the dramatic crisis. With its conflict-ridden characters and pungent language which shocked teachers, it gripped 16-year-old audiences, who could then see the point of discussing larger issues of freedom, responsibility, and sexual equality.

A three-year pilot project called "Living Together," initiated on the island of Gotland between 1973 and 1976 was designed by the Health Education Committee to "try out a method for health education in which the question of birth control is presented in the wider context of sexuality and human relations."[8] Gotland, about 100 miles long, with a population of 55,000 is a former Baltic shipping center, now largely agricultural, still characterized by extended families and strongly rooted traditional ideas, rather isolated from the mainstream of Swedish life. It has a higher than average teenage population, and in 1973 it had a higher teenage abortion rate than other rural counties: 28 per thousand women aged 14 to 19, compared to 20 per thousand elsewhere. Contraceptive services were available only at the maternal-health center of the county hospital. They were not considered an important part of the gynecological service.

The team from the National Board of Health and Welfare spent the entire first year of the project making contact with local decision makers, gaining the cooperation of the local school authorities, and establishing a working group including, among others, a midwife, a county school inspector, the island's two gynecologists, and a school psychologist. Long interviews were conducted with people whose work brought them into close contact with the intimate problems of families.

> It was clear from the initial interviews with key persons on Gotland that sexuality and childbirth had given rise to large, unmentionable problems. Welfare officers, midwives and doctors had felt powerless to tackle the shame connected with abortion, the tragedy of unwanted pregnancies and the multitude of sexual problems.[9]

The situation on Gotland was analyzed and a plan of activity drawn up. While this was going on, the contraceptive service was decentralized to the island's eight maternal-health centers and the district midwives were trained as counselors. Women no longer had to leave the children and farm animals and spend the day traveling to the county capital and back.

In the second year the project concentrated on getting information to professionals whose work involved problems of sexuality and human relations. Five five-day residential courses were given for 170 men and women from the health service, the schools, the social services, the church, local organizations, and the media. The participants not only listened to experts, they were led to examine their own attitudes, and the foundations were also laid for future cooperation among professionals who had previously worked along their own individual lines.

"You don't get any revolutionary results, but I assure you people do change," Hanna Olsson recalls. "When somebody says something out loud that you haven't ever dared say, it's some sort of a relief. You think, 'Well, it isn't any more dangerous than that!'"

Subsequently some members of this group were recruited as study circle leaders, and after five pilot circles proved successful the scheme was taken over by the local association for adult education. During the third year of the project thirty study circles were held which succeeded in involving people of all ages, including parents, teachers, teenagers in youth centers, young couples, and young men doing their army service.

The wisdom of getting in touch with journalists at an early stage and involving them in courses and other activity so that they could clarify their own attitudes proved itself in the generally serious, nonsensational coverage given the project in the local press. Two journalists who belonged to the original working group took over the task of carrying the project's message first to committees and boards, conferences and meetings, and later to school classes, talking about sex roles, contraceptives, about relations among young people and between them and the adult world, and about the influence of the media. They were also responsible for preparing the first material for the study circles, a 32-page illustrated tabloid in which informative articles based on the lectures given by experts at the five-day courses were interspersed with feature stories and interviews drawn from life on Gotland, together with practical information on where to turn for advice and guidance on personal problems.

Four independent theatre groups put on a total of 60 performances for schools and parents, featuring the conflicts between teenagers and adults on questions of "morality." One such play created a political row when the local board of education split along party lines over whether it should be allowed to go on, one side charging that the language was the kind scribbled on public walls and the other holding that it was in fact teenagers' everyday speech and would carry the message better than the mumblings of some teachers. Most of the performances were judged successful in breaking down inhibitions and thus helping to bridge the generation gap. As the members of one theatre group summed it up, "The people in the audience can see themselves without having to talk about themselves. They can talk in the third person, get a discussion going." [10]

All these activities stimulated more, which spread in ever-wider circles like "rings on the water" as the Health Education Committee had hopefully anticipated. Meetings, talks, and weekend courses were sponsored by various local agencies. A summer camp for 100 women and 40 children was so popular that it was repeated the following year. More men's groups were formed on Gotland than in any other part of Sweden. In the end, the Gotland Committee for Good Human Relations was formed, representing 22 women's and 16 youth groups, and received funds to support new local initiatives when the official project ended in 1976.

Summing up, the Health Education Committee attributed to the "Living Together" project the fact that Gotland alone among Swedish counties had in 1976 reached and surpassed the goal of 500 consultations per 1,000 women aged 14 to 44. Two-fifths of those seeking advice were under 20. While the number of abortions for

Sweden as a whole had leveled off at 32,000 or 20 per 1,000 women in the fertile age group, on Gotland the rate had dropped from 19 to 16, and for teenagers alone from 28 to 20. Births to teenagers had dropped as well. What the Gotland project had accomplished, through continuous discussion, was the creation of an atmosphere in which more and more people felt free to bring up questions they had never dared face before. A problem it raised but did not answer was "how the work should be arranged so that men not only become involved but can be induced to express their involvement in action."[11]

For the last few years, in line with a national decision to decentralize the work of central agencies, the Health Education Committee has been passing on its experiences to county councils, helping them to analyze their situations and to draw up plans. Six counties, for example, already have adopted "sexuality and human relations" programs long the lines of the Gotland project, and others are interested. Not all are so receptive, however. According to Gunilla Hollander:

> We had great interest in our work from 1975 to 1978. Then things changed. The labor market isn't so anxious for women anymore. There are very few children being born in Sweden. The power in the county councils is in the hands of men and we have to fight them all the time. They connect contraceptives with the fact that there are so few children, but the birthrate actually went up on Gotland during our project. We know that there are other reasons for not having children.

It's no longer just a question of preventing abortions, in her opinion:

> There is a new discussion of sexuality going on in Sweden. In the sixties we talked a lot about freedom and the possibility for women to have a free sexual life. Many people used this possibility, and it got a lot of treatment in the press. We know now that you cannot use your sexual freedom if you don't have freedom in your own role, and Swedish society is very far from that. If women don't get jobs and if they are not free economically they have to go back into the family. Young girls who can't find employment choose to have a child to give themselves identity. But at the same time you have a new woman in Sweden. She

wants to have her own life and she doesn't want to have children unless she has day care and other supports from society. We want the Equality Committee to do more to make people aware of these connections. The politicians don't see them.

While the health authorities have concentrated on expanding information to adults, in a parallel effort by the National Board of Education sex education in the schools has been overhauled. While one commission was preparing a new abortion law, another was reviewing what children were being taught.

Compulsory sex education had been introduced in the schools in 1956, and by the 1960s Sweden was already well ahead of other countries in its ideas of what young children ought to know. As an American professor of family life, Lester A. Kirkendall of the University of Oregon, noted in 1966 in his introduction to *Sex and Society in Sweden* by Birgitta Linnér, a Swedish authority on sex education:

> American public opinion for some time now has regarded the Swedes as "promiscuous," and, naturally, as less virtuous than ourselves. . . . We concentrate grimly and intently upon what proportion of our young people engage in premarital intercourse, and assume that feminine virtue depends upon virginity. We begin with thinking about the sex act, we fix our concern at that point, and often never get beyond it.[12]

The Swedish purpose was to remove the secrecy surrounding sexual relations and present them as a natural part of life, with the idea that informed individuals would be able to make mature and responsible personal decisions. Children aged seven to nine not only learned in school how a baby was born but, at the discretion of the teacher, were told about sexual intercourse. Children ten to twelve (boys and girls together) discussed masturbation, menstruation, and contraception. A 1966 book used for 14–17 year olds, which also was the basic text for a TV course, expected pupils to know which three contraceptive techniques were safest, and which one was most suitable for teenagers. At this age they were also taught that attitudes toward homosexuality have varied from culture to culture, that in Sweden homosexual relations between consenting adults had not been considered illegal since 1944 although considerable prejudice still existed, and that such noted personalities as Michelangelo and Tchaikovsky were homosexuals.

The children got the facts: this was the positive side of the picture according to Birgitta Linnér. The negative side was that there was too much reliance on biology textbooks, too much moralizing, and too little said about the complexity of personal relationships. There was no compulsory training for teachers themselves in sex education. Children were told that the one acceptable reason for sexual relations was reproduction, extramarital relations were ruled out in favor of early marriage, and the realities of Swedish life were ignored. The double standard was never mentioned. The official handbook of the Board of Education on the subject of sex education advised that pregnant schoolgirls should be removed from the class before their condition became visible, for their own good and that of other pupils.

In this the school reflected the influence of the many who continued to believe that the focus of sex education should be the home, that premarital sex should never be condoned, and that information about contraception encouraged promiscuity. One hundred and forty Swedish doctors petitioned the government for a stricter approach to sexual norms in teaching, and 200,000 churchwomen from all over the country presented a similar appeal. Meanwhile more and younger children were being exposed to the media and were aware that what they were being told in school was not what was being practiced in the adult world. While in 1971 a survey showed that 70 percent of parents of teenagers still wanted total abstinence for their sons and daughters, 75 percent of Swedish youngsters had had intercourse in their teens.

The government commission in its 1974 report, 800 pages long and based on 10 years of investigation and deliberation, took note of this conflict of values, but also pointed out that many parents had no objection to their teenage children "going steady," even if it involved living together, provided they acted in a responsible way. The commission gave its opinion that "It would be wrong in principle and fatal to teaching if the school were morally to reject these young people and their parents. The attitude of the school cannot be decided by reference to a majority."[13] The report proposed that teachers "start from the factual circumstances" that the most usual motive for sex is pleasure rather than propagation. It suggested that "the excessively early sexual relationships that occur should be combated by other aspects of teaching than a general recommendation of restraint while one is young."[14] The handbook for teachers based on this report advises teachers not to counsel young people to marry early rather than engage in a premarital relationship. "Panegyrics to marriage" have been replaced by emphasis on the importance of lasting personal relationships. While the previous handbook instructed teachers to "strongly emphasize" that contraceptives give only relative protection, this is omitted in the new version since it is no longer true and could lead pupils to believe that it is not worthwhile to use contraceptives. Emphasis is placed on the need for taking a firm stand on certain moral values: support for the integrity of the individual (no one is simply an object for another person's pleasure), consideration for others (one does not expose others to the dangers of pregnancy or VD); the equality of women and men in sexual relationships as elsewhere. Teachers are also enjoined to give a fair presentation of conflicting views on such subjects as abortion, birth control, and premarital sex.

The present syllabus has advanced the subject matter so that sex education begins at the preschool level, where children learn some basic facts about their bodies and find out where babies come from. For pupils 13 to 16, sex education is divided among various courses, so that the biological, psychological, ethical, and social aspects are covered in the context of science and the humanities. A textbook by Birgitta Linnér for secondary schools and parent education, titled *Family and Psychological Relationships*, attempts to integrate sex education and sex-role equality into the realities of everyday life in a variety of cultures. It also deals with the psychological aspects of both homosexual and heterosexual relationships, with communal living, and with one-parent families. At this early adolescent level the school may make use of seminars, panel discussions, and outside experts.

This is the present model of sex instruction which is still too new to have had a fundamental impact on the attitudes of today's teenagers. In the experience of Hollander and others directly concerned with the consequences of sexual mores—including the recent increase in teenage prostitution—the past stress on information without sufficient guidance concerning how to use it has not helped young people to form a code of behavior that could lead to the lasting warmth and affection they are seeking. "At most we've been telling them that it doesn't hurt to wait until you're eighteen," one observer has wryly commented. "Perhaps there is something called love we ought to be talking about."

How does respect for the identity of the individual and condemnation of the use of persons of either sex simply to fulfill the needs of another square with a permissive attitude toward the commercial exploitation of sex? Sweden's view today is that behavior that is morally repugnant to many is not necessarily criminal, and consequently sexual acts performed between consenting adults are not punishable. Moreover, it is argued, sexual activity now begins so young, and premarital relations are so ubiquitous that it is difficult to decide where "morality" leaves off and crime begins. Thus prostitution, exhibitionism, and incest—behavior which historically speaking the law has proved powerless to stop—are no longer part of the penal code. There are not, however, officially licensed brothels as there are in West Germany and Holland, for example. Procuring, including renting rooms to people who meet for casual sexual contacts, sexual molestation of children, sexual relations with children under 14 or with one's own child under the age of 18, and acts of sexual coercion are punishable with prison terms. For the most serious crime of coercion, rape, offenders may be sentenced to from two to ten years.

The regulation of sex clubs and "posing studios" is governed by the philosophy that people should be allowed the widest possible latitude in choosing their activities. At the same time it is felt that these pornographic shows provide a favorable milieu for asocial and criminal activities. They are therefore allowed only by permission of the police authorities, which theoretically at least gives the police control over their criminal misuse. At the orginary nightspot everything is antiseptically wrapped. "Naked girls dance on customers' tables but are safe from reach behind glass cages," if one is to believe the SAS flight magazine, which provided this reassurance in its issue for October 1979 in an article entitled "Protecting Swedish Consumers." By voluntary agreement, the Swedish Newspaper Publishers' Association does not publish advertisements with provocative sex illustrations or those that solicit clients for "posing studios" or other thinly veiled invitations to meet prostitutes.

One area in which neither the rational arguments of the government health and education authorities nor the pressure of women's organizations has been effective is the extent of pornography in the mass media itself, and especially in the slick magazines. "It's increasing. You can't appeal to the publishers," according to Gunilla Hollander. "We've tried it. They agree that what we have to say is interesting, but there's too much money in it." This controversy reveals at its most poignant a danger lurking behind "the right to be human," with its assumption that both men and women are equally victims of patriarchal society and share an interest in fighting it. There is a temptation to adopt the convention that the oppressor is impersonal; it is "the system" and not the male sex. It may be assumed for the sake of possibly fruitful negotiations that the managers of industry or the union leaders can be persuaded to take steps toward the more equal division of sex roles that they claim to favor. One can obtain certain concrete gains that can be used as a wedge, which will in turn help to change attitudes, and thus eventually arrive at a new position from which a new strategy can be tried. In this area it is possible to reduce sex-role inequality to a concept, and to discuss it impersonally, as an institution that both men and women would like to see changed.

When the issue is pornography, however, biological considerations that the sex-role debate regards as irrelevant suddenly define the point of view, and the inequality of the two "victims" is exposed. What appears to one negotiator as an abstract consumer product or a symbol of freedom of the press appears to the other as an act of sexual oppression and exploitation of women by men. One of the negotiators is being sold to the other (in effigy) in the most humiliating circumstances possible, and is being asked at the same time to recognize that this is good business and will even contribute funds to the public sector to continue the fight against sado-masochistic models of sex relations. The Health Education Committee, like Sisyphus, continues to push its stone toward the top of the hill in the knowledge that more powerful forces have an interest in sending it back.

Notes

1. This quotation is drawn from Rita Liljeström, Gunilla Fürst Mellström, and Gillan Liljeström Svensson, *Roles in Transition* (Stockholm: Liber Förlag, 1978), pp. 98-99. Those above are from personal interviews.

2. Christopher Tietze and Marjorie Cooper Murstein, "Induced Abortion: 1975 Factbook," *Reports on Population/Family Planning* (New York: The Population Council, 1975), tables 2b and 2c, pp. 18-22.

3. The Soviet Union restricted the right to abortion in 1936, making it a criminal offense, "except for compelling medical and eugenic reasons," then liberalized its abortion law again in 1955. For a full discussion see Henry P. David, *Family Planning and Abortion in the Socialist Countries of Central and Eastern Europe* (New York: The Population Council, 1970), chapter 2.

4. Lawrence Lader, *Abortion II: Making the Revolution* (Boston: Beacon Press, 1973), p. 35.

5. Quoted in Rita Liljeström, *A Study of Abortion in Sweden* (Stockholm: Allmänna Förlaget, 1974), p. 43.

6. From the English summary to the report of the parliamentary committee set up to review the question of therapeutic abortions, published as *Rätten Till Abort* (Stockholm, 1971) (SOU:1971:58).

7. *Living Together: A Family Planning Project on Gotland, Sweden 1973-1976* (Stockholm: Committee on Health Education, National Swedish Board of Health and Welfare, 1978), p. 12.

8. Ibid., p. 68.

9. Ibid., p. 47.

10. Ibid., p. 32.

11. Ibid., p. 64.

12. Lester A. Kirkendall, preface to B. Linnér, *Sex and Society in Sweden* (New York: Harper Colophon, 1972), p. x.

13. Report of the government commission on sex education, *Sexual— och samlevnadsundervisning* (Stockholm: Liber Förlag, 1974)(SOU:1974:59), p. 809 (English summary).

14. Ibid., p. 804.

CHAPTER 6

Rejoining the Child and Adult Worlds

"Why didn't the kings come?" was a banner headline in the Stockholm *Expressen* on October 19, 1979. The accompanying photograph presented two of the world's most photogenic queens smiling at one of the most photogenic scenes that a Swedish day-care center can provide: two-year-olds playing naked in water in a plastic-lined room especially designed for the purpose. The queens were the Swedish Silvia and the Spanish Sofia. The missing kings were Spain's Juan Carlos and his host, Sweden's Carl Gustaf, who had gone instead to examine cables and other communications equipment at L. M. Ericsson.

"It's a shame," the *Expressen* quoted Birgitta Wistrand, president of the Fredrika Bremer Association, as saying.

Society gives millions to break down sex roles, and then the royal idols do just the opposite. They are the models who ought to do better. . . . We have a modern queen, and in spite of that the day before yesterday the "boys" went to the Academy of Sciences and the "girls" went to look at beautiful things. The kings have children too.

Asked to comment, a spokesman at the Royal Court replied, "We can't sit here chatting about boys' and girls' programs when such an important thing as Swedish exports is at stake." The Spanish market, he said, was too vital. Besides, the King had visited a day nursery.

The woman reporter who made the front page with this message about the realities of Swedish life had an unbeatable combination in Queen Silvia and day care—two sure-fire subjects for journalistic exploitation in Sweden. While queens everywhere are always good for a story and always have been, intense public interest in day care is something of a Swedish specialty and is relatively recent.

Sweden has been among the laggards in Western Europe in providing care outside the home for its preschool children. In 1977–78 it could provide for only 13 percent of its three-year-olds, 17 percent of four-year-olds, and 33 percent of five-year-olds (see Table 7). This put it not only far behind such leaders as Belgium and France, which are approaching total coverage for children aged three to six, but in arrears of most of the other countries on the European continent. The gap is all the more worthy of note in the light of the very high percentage of gainfully employed Swedish mothers (68 percent in 1978) with children under seven.

In Sweden's defense it must be said that it is almost impossible to arrive at truly comparable cross-national statistics on day care. In Table 6.1, compiled from the results of a questionnaire circulated to national authorities by the Council of Europe, Sweden's figures represent full-time, state-subsidized places in day-care centers under the supervision of a single government agency. Some other countries' figures include nursery schools and nursery classes which do not give all-day care and do not always even include a midday meal. For example, as the United Kingdom's Equal Opportunities Commission noted in September 1978: "In Great Britain there is no coherent or systematic provision for the day care needs of families with preschool children." Almost all of the available care is part time.[1] The United States does not have a clearly delineated system of care; most day-care arrangements "are under proprietary (for profit) auspices."[2] A further handicap, which Sweden shares with the other Scandinavian countries except for Iceland, is that preschool care must cover six-year-olds, since the school-starting age is seven.

None of these mitigating circumstances can disguise the fact that Sweden entered the field with considerable delay. Austria, Belgium, Germany, and France laid the foundation for their present strong position in the mid-nineteenth century, when officially recognized *crèches* and *Krippen* were established with pedagogical goals outlined by the psychologists Pestalozzi and Froebel. These ideas reached Sweden as well, but did not find the same response in a primarily rural society. In 1938, as one of the series of Population Commission reports, Alva Myrdal, in collaboration with a medical adviser, prepared recommendations for state-subsidized preschool institutions, pointing not only to the social and educational value of day nurseries for children but to the freedom they would give mothers. It may have been just this threat to the cultural pattern which assumed woman's chief role to be that of childminder that backfired, for no action was taken on the proposal. Again in 1951 a new government commission suggested that the municipalities increase the availability of day care, but for 15 years almost nothing happened; the number of places grew only from 10,000 to 12,000.

The commission's recommendations coincided with the Bowlby Report of the World Health Organization, presenting evidence to support a supposed irreversible emotional damage in young children separated from their mothers. This gave, as Sture Henricsson, one of the authors of Sweden's present Preschool Act, puts it, "a scientific framework to people's prejudices. At the central government level day care continued to be discussed, but in the municipalities it wasn't an issue. No one even thought about it."

In Sweden, as in most other Western industrialized states, the selection by the experts of the mother-child dyad as the necessary starting point for all research on child development, and the idealization of the full-time mother by the lay public, continued throughout the fifties and early sixties to block new avenues of approach to children's needs. It hardly seems coincidental that a change of views concerning the mother's function and the child's place in society came with the demand for women workers as the service sector in the industrial countries began to undergo rapid expansion. Economic pressure was on the side of those who had begun to question the "deprivation syndrome." Interest was revived in role theory, developed in the United States by social psychologist George Herbert Mead in the twenties and thirties, and in the experimental work of Jean Piaget, the Swiss psychologist, in tracing the cognitive development of children. Mead's proposition that social roles are learned through play and Piaget's view of the importance of children for other children in forming their understanding of the world helped to create a concept of preschool institutions as not just social services, but crucial environments for the development of the child's personality and capacity to learn.

This trend of thought has gathered strength in Scandinavia. As can be seen in Table 6.1, Sweden, Norway, and Iceland are, with France, the only West European countries devoting resources to facilities for children under three years of age. In some other countries policies are actively directed to keeping children of this age at home. Austria, for example, replied to the Council of Europe questionnaire that "as a rule . . . children develop best when they stay with their mothers," and consequently it restricts day nurseries for the youngest group of children to "extreme cases of emergency." The Federal Republic of Germany also contends that young children should be placed in day care only when there are strong social reasons.[3] This view is shared by a number of East European countries which use a flat cash allowance to encourage the care of the small child at home. Thus Sweden, which in 1978 had 14 percent of its under-threes in either day care or state-approved family day care, ranked ahead of Czechoslovakia with 8 percent and Hungary with 10 percent, although far behind the German Democratic Republic with 50 percent of this age group accommodated.

Not that this positive view of day care for the very young took hold in Sweden immediately and universally. In the mid-sixties the Family Welfare Committee recommended a childcare allowance on the grounds that it would allow the mother to stay at home, or at least give her "freedom to choose" whether to do so. As has been seen, the childcare allowance is still strongly favored by the Center and Conservative parties today. It was primarily the Social Democratic women's organization, under pressure from other women and especially from young parents, and with the aid of a strong-minded Minister of Family Affairs, Camilla Odhnoff, now chairperson of the Family Aid Commission, which succeeded in creating a political atmosphere favorable to the development of day care as an essential support for sex-role equality. Once this was established, experts undertook a review of the psychological and medical arguments for and against day nurseries for very young children. Kerstin Sjöblom, a child psychologist and Research Director of the Family Aid Commission, which acts as an investigative body for the National Board of Health and Welfare, recalls that it took her months of sitting in nurseries, studying the relationship of infants to the personnel, to notice the "very great pleasure these infants took in looking at each other and trying to play with each other." She had never dreamed of putting her own three children in a day nursery, preferring to entrust them to a family day-care mother. "I was so convinced by all the theories I had read that I thought babies didn't derive any benefit at all from contact with other babies."

Today the Family Aid Commission states firmly:

> Studies carried out during the past ten or fifteen years unanimously suggest that even very small children establish social relationships with each other and benefit from associating with each other. . . . Practically all investigations suggest that day nursery children are particularly favoured in terms of social, emotional and intellectual development and in the development of independence and initiative.[4]

On the question of the high illness rate among very small children attending day-care centers, which is often raised by opponents of day care for this age group, Swedish investigators agree that it is high, but say that a small percentage of children account for most of the days lost through illness. According to a survey of 8,000 preschool children made in 1974, almost half were never ill while at the other extreme 18 percent missed nearly one-quarter of all school days. Those children who are especially prone to illness probably do better in the smaller groups supervised by a family day-care mother, who can take care of no more than six children (including her own) in her own home. This has somewhat strengthened interest in family day care, which has not been considered by Swedish authorities to provide as good an environment as day-care centers. Some municipalities have increased their support for day-care mothers and are trying to integrate their work with that of the municipally run nurseries. The main result of the survey, however, was the extension of the parental leave for the care of a sick child at home to 60 days annually per child per family.

Findings in other areas supported the arguments for expanding day care for younger as well as older preschool children. A study on the total environment of children made by Bror Rexed, the Director of the National Board of Health and Welfare, in the early seventies revealed that in spite of the many across-the-board benefits aimed at children, there were still big differences when it came to the start in life that Swedish families at various social levels could give their youngsters. The highest income groups had twice the resources available for family consumption as the lowest and 50 percent more than the middle income brackets. While only 15 percent of Swedish families were overcrowded in the sense that they had less than one room per family member (kitchen excluded), half of the "overcrowded" families had several children and were in the lowest income group.[5]

A second general experience that influenced the expansion of day care was gained from the Swedish school reform of the sixties. It confirmed the findings in other countries: equal opportunity does not create equality. Equal access to education does not benefit everyone equally. As Annika Baude, an expert at the National Board of Health and Welfare, has observed:

> The school, it became clear, was not succeeding in compensating children for an unsatisfactory environment during their preschool years. It was hoped, therefore, that by expanding preschool programs there would be a better chance to achieve the goal of equality to which politicians were committed.[6]

A third argument came out of the sex-role debate. This arose from the discovery that the mere elimination of formal sex barriers in education, the introduction of a uniform elementary-school curriculum for girls and boys, and attention given to sex-role issues in classroom discussion had not affected the traditional choices of young people. This point was made in a report to the Nordic Council of Ministers by an intergovernmental committee on sex roles and education in 1972:

> Our present system of education does not contribute to greater equality between the sexes. . . . Traditional sex roles have a strong hold and alter very slowly in education as in society in general. Scarcely any attempt has been made to remove the great differences which still exist, not only in the conditions of life but also in personality development and attitudes. . . . Preschools offer the best opportunity of combating those early differences in the personality development of the sexes which have a lasting influence, and such schools are also a necessity if parents with young children are to be able to work.[7]

The combination of all these factors created the attitudes necessary for change. The trade unions put their weight behind day care. In 1973 Parliament passed the Preschool Activities Act by a large majority. The new law placed the responsibility for developing day care on the municipalities, with part of the initial cost and the operating expenses met by the central government.

Priority at the start was to be given to providing care for six year olds and for the children of parents who were working or studying. The law stipulated that beginning in July 1975 at least part-time care must be provided for all six year olds and those four- and five-year-olds who for physical, mental, social, or linguistic reasons were in special need of support. (Linguistic support is needed especially by that 7 percent of children whose parents are immigrants, mostly Finnish but some Yugoslav and other minorities.) In addition to meeting this need, the municipalities were instructed to draw up annual sliding five-year plans covering future expansion of day care and other out-of-school activities.

It soon became obvious that things were moving at a snail's pace, and that the "old men in the municipal councils" were sitting on their hands. Demonstrations and marches for day care became part of the scene. The first parents' pressure group for day care was formed in Örebro, an industrial city in central Sweden, and succeeded in preventing threatened cuts in day-care spending after the local Social Democratic government was voted out of office. Politicians were forced to debate their opinion of nursery schools as an unnecessary expense with parents, teachers, doctors, and psychologists. In Social Democratic Stockholm a storm broke in the municipal council. The plan for 1975 projected a number of day-care places that was less than the number of families on the waiting list—which was already longer than the previous year in spite of the new places that had been added. All the Social Democratic members of Stockholm city and regional councils were sent out to visit day-care centers, and many of them succeeded in getting their pictures in the paper promising a drastic search for new premises.

Finally convinced that state intervention was required, Parliament approved a plan for 100,000 new day-care places and 50,000 places in leisure-time centers between 1977 and 1981, which amounted to doubling the plans that had been put forward by the municipalities. It was estimated that this would cover the needs of 80 percent of preschool children with working mothers. In addition, by the end of the five-year period all six-year-olds and all four- and five-year-olds at risk would have at least part time care.

Although day care is now the largest single item on most municipalities' budgets and the pressure of parents wanting places for their children continues, it appears that the target will not be reached before the end of 1982. The coalition government's stress on alternative forms of support for childcare in the home, plus the impact of inflation and recession on all expenditures, has encouraged some municipal governments to whittle down their day-care estimates. If present projections turn out to be correct, by December 1983 there will be places for 28 percent of all preschool children in day-care centers, and another 14 percent will be accommodated in supervised family day-care in private homes. Some 17 percent of children aged 7—12 will have access to after-school care either in a leisure-time center or in a family day-care group. (The percentages are helped along by the fact that the number of children born each year in Sweden is declining: from 729,400 in 1978 to a projected 684,400 in 1983.)

Figures vary from one part of Sweden to another. In Stockholm, for example, the situation is better than the average for the country as a whole. One reason, according to Stockholm welfare authorities, is that most municipalities plan on the basis of their waiting list while Stockholm plans on the solidly grounded assumption that many more women would apply if more places were available. Thus Stockholm plans officially to have 72 percent of its preschool children in day care by 1985 and another 8 percent in family day care, but expects realistically to reach this target much sooner. Throughout the country, it is hoped, demand for places will be covered by 1985—86.

"If the communities don't keep their promises we'll have to resort to more legislation," according to Gabriel Romanus, a Liberal MP.

Rapid expansion has had to be accompanied by the establishment of standards that advance the stated goal of preschool education as "an entirely necessary support to the child's long-term development into a mature adult, who can function both as an independent individual and in cooperation and interplay with others as a democratic human being."[8] Numerous recommendations brought in by the original Commission on Child Centers as the basis for the Preschool Activities Act and by its successor, the Family Aid Commission, have been tested to create the present Swedish model.

The aim is an institution that contributes to, among other goals, a more equal division of roles between women and men, first by providing care for the children of working parents and second by actively working to break down stereotyped behavior by its own structure and educational content. This purpose is not consistent with a neutral stand in the day-care vs. childcare-allowance debate. The Family Aid Commission has taken a position against proposals for giving parents who care for their children at home the same financial advantages (by paying them a childcare subsidy) as those who use subsidized day care. The "freedom of choice" argument advanced in favor of these proposals is a false one, in the opinion of commission chairperson Camilla Odhnoff, because "freedom of choice is a reality only for women in families with good incomes, and this represents only a small part of the population." This is not to say that the commission belittles parental care. On the contrary, its proposals (so far not adopted) have included compulsory participation by the father in any extension of parental leave, compulsory parental education, compensation to parents of small children who voluntarily reduce their working time, and paid time-off to parents to participate in preschool activities. Odhnoff has made plain that in her opinion the top decision makers in government, business, and the unions are men who are blind to certain problems because they never come in contact with them:

> We are well aware that our proposals ask a great deal of the labor market in the way of organizational structure and administrative procedures, (but) we must take the consequences of the fact that our welfare is based on the work of both men and women. From this it follows that the job world must own up to the awkward fact that there are children in our society and that both fathers and mothers may sometimes have legitimate reasons for putting the interests of children ahead of the job world.[9]

Great stress in the Swedish preschool is laid upon team work by the staff to break down the hierarchy of director—preschool teacher—children's nurse—cook and to counteract the messages of a competitive society, divided by age and social category, with the possibility of cooperation and solidarity. The daily routine is characterized by give and take between children and adults, with the aim of helping children through a continuing dialogue to form a clear sense of their own identity, to develop their own values and their ability to communicate. It strives to achieve an atmosphere of emotional openness in which people feel free to show their feelings. The play program is a highly unstructured one in which children can work on a project, read, listen to a story, take part in active games or sleep, without disrupting a group schedule.

Two innovations of potential significance for a more equal division of sex roles have been the introduction of mixed age groups and the employment of male preschool teachers.

About half of Swedish day-care centers divide the children so that 12 children under three make up one group while 15 to 18 aged three to seven make up another. The recommended staff ratio is two for each five children in the younger group and one for every five in the older. The national average is one staff member for 4.7 children, including cooks and cleaners, which is high in comparison with other countries. This high density of personnel itself implies acceptance of the idea that day care is an irreplaceable supplement to family care, even for children under two.

Experience with these mixed-age groups, and especially with the older "sibling groups" has been favorable. This is a family-type experience that is lacking in the growing number of one-child families. The membership in the group remains relatively stable, so that children's friendships and their relationship with the staff have greater continuity. It promotes a sense of responsibility in the older children, and is a natural way of introducing boys to child care.

According to Karen Blomqvist, Secretary of the Family Aid Commission, recent experiments in a few centers provide encouragement for the idea of expanding groups to take in the whole age range of preschool children and even to include younger school children as well:

> We've known for some time now that the little children learn from each other. What is interesting is that not only do the small children learn from the older ones, but the older children become very attached to the younger ones and so are able to use their whole register of emotions.

A convincing example of this reported by one experimental center was the experience of a school-age boy who had taken a one-year-old girl under his wing and insisted on her sharing the benefits of a trip to the museum. Although this wasn't part of the plan, the staff decided to be flexible and the boy had the main responsibility for his charge throughout the excursion, to his great satisfaction.

Most of the problems arising out of the mixed-age arrangements result from the fact that, because of the shortage of day care, many of those who receive places are priority children requiring special care. When very small children are added to the group it may create a difficult situation. The only solution, according to Blomqvist, is to meet the demand for day care:

> We find that quality depends on interaction among children of different ages, so that for us you are not solving the situation by keeping the child home for more than a year. Even the very small children need to meet other children and other grown ups. You're not doing either the adult or the child any good by making them stay home and cutting off relationships.

The employment of men in nursery school posts is one of the few Swedish successes in breaking down the stereotyped division of employment. It also provides children with the model of a caretaking man as a natural phenomenon, which may be especially important for the many children from single-parent families headed by women who gain priority day-care places.

Georg, a teacher at a Stockholm day-care center which is used to test teaching practices, was one of four men in a teachers' training class of 25. He went into it because he wanted to work with people and he realized that you have to start early if you want to "create a free person who is independent and at the same time can help others."

In his school there are three groups, one of 14 of the youngest children, and two "sibling groups" of 18 children each. Georg is one of five—two teachers and three child nurses—taking care of those aged seven months to two-and-a-half years.

> It's harder to work with mixed ages, but it's much better because you have an atmosphere of working together instead of different age groups competing. For instance, I have three children and they are "mine." Every time they have to be changed, I do it, and when they eat I'm there. The children get the feeling, well he's here, I'm safe." If they come when they are seven or eight months old, I'm their person until they are two and a half. When they get to the brother-and-sister group they are ready to cooperate because they already have that feeling of security.

The reservation of a limited number of places for men in preschool teacher training is the only example of the use of quotas in the Swedish educational system. Since 1971, 10 percent of places have been set aside for promising male applicants who did not have the necessary formal qualifications to enter the two-year post-secondary school course. The other places were open to both sexes on the same basis. This quota system is likely to be dropped because the union objects that it tends to squeeze women out of one of the few professions open to them. Some of those involved in the program believe that it is no longer necessary to encourage men to enter in this way; less than 15 percent of men students in the day-care course now take advantage of the quota. Others believe that male participation is leveling off. At present men account for about 4 percent of preschool teachers and 10 percent of teachers-in-training.

Will men stay in preschool teaching after the novelty wears off? Georg says for himself:

> Well, I hope so. But I was brought up to be a man, and I have this career idea in my mind. It's there. My mother and father, they say you have got to get a real job. And I don't want to be like that because I really enjoy this work, but my surroundings are telling me of course you should be—well, you shouldn't stay there. Work with children? It couldn't be! It's a woman's job!

Does he try to persuade his men friends to go into this work?

> Daily. Just being, I think. Doing. People are realizing.

Do his friends think it's funny?

> No, they envy me. They respect me. I haven't met one single man who's told me "that's ridiculous." Sometimes they get very embarrassed because their man's role is threatened. They can't talk "man to man" with me. So they are silent, and then suddenly they ask me well, tell me man, uh, how is it? There must be something in it because he's not stupid, they say. What is it? It's very important that you talk in a job like this, thereby creating a new situation for men.

The actual educational impact of male teachers in the preschools has not yet been evaluated. So far it has not been observed that they leave to take better jobs or that they are the ones who rise to administrative posts in the educational hierarchy, but this may be because they have not been around long enough to acquire seniority. What has been discovered is that male preschool teachers play out their conventional roles in their unconventional jobs. They continue to represent sport and science, while the women teachers continue to represent food. If there is furniture to be moved, a repair to be made, a light bulb to be changed, it is the man who does it. According to Blomqvist this is particularly true when there is only one male teacher in a school. A film made by the Equality Committee at a school where the staff is divided 50–50 shows, however, that even here the traditional division of roles manages to survive. This film has been shown all over Sweden.

There is also evidence that although on the conscious level the preschool staffs try to counteract the traditional socialization of children by dividing the tasks, stressing the interchangeability of roles, leading the boys to cook and the girls to hammer nails, they do in fact make a distinction between girls and boys at the unconscious level. A study made in Göteborg has revealed that the staff reacts quite differently to each sex. The boys are left much more on their own, while the girls are closer to the personnel, receive more encouragement from them, and are stimulated to do things that the staff likes to do—which are usually "typically female." A wider use of male teachers might be a way of breaking this circle.

The place of day care in the wider context of a society in which women and men occupy more nearly equal roles is no longer a purely theoretical problem, now that it appears possible that a number of Western countries, Sweden included, will be able to satisfy the demand for day care by the end of the present decade. People whose blueprint for the future includes sex-role equality find it unrewarding to visualize a society in which tasks are divided in such a way that women learn to shoulder their way to the top like men, and men like women learn to juggle a dozen responsibilities at home and on the job and always manage to look fresh and appealing. A society organized on the principle of equality will use technology to allow more time for personal relations. Personal life and public life will no longer be two separate domains, one assigned primarily to women and the other to men, but the personal will become a legitimate part of the public. Above all, society will recognize that investment of both time and money in children is as important as investment in the production of goods—or even more so.

If this concept is to have any reality, it will mean breaking down the isolation of families as units that prepare their members for, or protect them against, contact with the "outside world" (meaning members of other families). The preschool may contribute to this by creating a democratic and less sex-stereotyped community for children, but at the cost of further isolating the child's world from that of adults. The "privatization of infancy" in Western society is drawing attention in a number of countries. As the French authors Schérer and Hocquenghem have commented:

> Nobody mixes with children any more. If you are not a father or a mother, that is, a possessor of children, if you do not belong to the family of watchdogs, psychologists or psychoanalysts, if you are only "a man without qualities," you will pass by children without ever having the occasion to really get to know one. You see them pass by, you meet them in the street or on the stairs. . . .[10]

An obvious way to begin to break down this isolation is by involving first parents in the life of the preschool and then by integrating day care in the life of the community. In the words of a report by the Swedish Family Aid Commission:

> The development of parental participation in day nurseries would give all children in the group access to a larger number of adults, both men and women. . . . Cooperation between parents and staff and between parents themselves can mark the beginning of combined efforts to transform the conditions of the individual, of the day nursery and of the housing area as a whole. . . . The social isolation of day nurseries can be broken by means of increased parental participation.[11]

Sweden, by the admission of its day-care authorities, does not have ideal conditions for parent participation. One of the by-products of welfare state, as has often been noted, is that there are so many official agencies whose paid job it is to deal with social problems, that the individual tends to pay less and less attention to the neighbors' troubles. Since in Sweden the welfare state has coincided with almost the entire period of intensive industrialization and urbanization, a tradition of volunteer work has never developed. In the schools, for example, there are parents' groups but nothing to correspond, in activity and influence, to the Parents' and Teachers' Association in the United States. In the preschool there has been emphasis on achieving a standard level of staff qualifications throughout Sweden, and parents are not present as helpers as they often are in Great Britain.[12] With almost all preschool parents employed, and with demands on them to take part in trade-union education and to become involved in decision making at their place of work, the time left for involvement in the children's world is shrinking.

Some experiments in parent participation are presently under way. At one cooperative day-care center (of which there are very few in Sweden) parents have on their own initiative decided to work in the school an average of one and a half days per month. This is a condition for membership. A preschool teacher, a child nurse, and two parents are always on duty. The parents put in all their time at a stretch or divide it in any way that fits into the schedule. The municipality reimburses parents for their time at the going rate for child nurses. This scheme has attracted considerable interest. The last six months of the present twelve-month "parental leave," which may now be used in a flexible way over a number of years, provide time for this kind of activity, theoretically, at least. Because of the shortage of day-care places, however, most parents must in practice take their twelve months of leave consecutively. As in the case of the successful use of mixed-age groups, the involvement of parents in day care is seen as depending on adequate day-care coverage and the reduction of the working day.

An innovative way of joining the preschool with the community is the open preschool. This was introduced in Sweden in 1972 with the idea of giving children for whom there are no day-care places available, or whose parents are at home, contact with other children in an educational setting, and at the same time of breaking down the isolation of parents and family day-care mothers.

The open preschool is equipped along the lines of a day-care center and has a preschool teacher in attendance. Toys and equipment are there to be used, but there is no planned program. The aim is contact, information, advice, and stimulation. It is a place where adults can meet other adults informally while their children play, and other activities may develop spontaneously out of these meetings.

Ideally the open preschool is located near other community social services such as the children's health center, so that parents find it convenient to drop in. The response has been very positive, and there are now 136 such preschools in Sweden. One, in the industrial town of Västerås, on a large housing estate with a considerable immigrant population, serves a catchment area with 650 children of preschool age. It employs social workers, nurses, and psychologists, and is developing an outreach program to involve prospective fathers and mothers.

A notably successful effort to involve the community in the child's world is coordinated by the Council for Children's Play, created within the National Board of Health and Welfare in 1971. This had its start in the international play movement, which grew in protest against the artificial and stereotyped character of children's playgrounds and has attempted to create real environments that encourage the child's initiative and provide a place where children and adults can do things together. Sweden has drawn particularly from the experience of Denmark, but also from West German and British models. An annual state grant administered by the National Housing Board is available to municipalities and property owners who will match state fund with their own to improve the residential environment. The idea is to get away from the standard slides and sandboxes and create natural meeting places for everyone in the area.

Recent legislation requires a play area and a common playground for every housing development with more than 30 units, and a municipal playground with trained personnel within 300 yards of housing areas with more than 150 families. Tenants may receive municipal funds to organize these activities themselves, as a result of which community centers with hobby workshops have been established in vacant flats, lawns have been turned into vegetable gardens, and play villages have been constructed by parents, pensioners, and teenagers. In one Stockholm suburb an old farmhouse was salvaged and restocked with animals to re-create a farm life which most city children know only from books. A manual on outdoor play and the local environment, written by an expert for the National Tenants' Association, has been studied by hundreds of tenants groups drawing up their own plans for improving their neighborhoods. By mid-1979 some 4,000 projects had been financed under this program.

All these measures, which are themselves in an early stage of development, stop at the threshold of a major problem which concerns child specialists in Sweden as in other countries. This is the decreasing opportunity for children to learn through actual experience. Viewed from the perspective of sex-role equality, what models are available to children? Children all over Europe, says Eva Nordland, a Norwegian educator, "are growing up in an environment devoid of events." Parents disappear into the unknown every day, necessities are purchased prepackaged, life on the housing estate or in the garden suburb stands still, play has no continuity with the child's future, fantasy roles are absorbed from the TV and comic books. She observes:

> In this connection, the play movement and the preschool movement do not have satisfactory answers to a major problem of children in the industrialised society. One of the long-term goals of schools as well as the play- and pre-school movements, should be to look for ways and means of reintegrating children into the life of their adults. . . .[13]

In Karen Blomqvist's view:

> The whole function of play as an aid to concept development is jeopardized. A child starts off bravely on its tricycle: "Now I'm going to work like Daddy." Then it stops short. What next? It has no idea of what Daddy does. We want to work with ways of giving children a chance to become part of the grown-up world so that play, which is the child's work, will not be separated from the real life of adults.

One possible approach being developed in a cross-disciplinary study in Göteborg suggests a reorganization of work that would give adults one day a week to use for work in their living area. Every day some familiar adults would be involved in community activity and could take their own and other children with them. A token step of this kind was initiated during one week of 1979, International Children's Year, on the suggestion of women in the white-collar trade unions. All workers and employees were urged to bring their children to "see what you do all day," and whole preschool classes invaded factory halls and the sanctuaries of re-research institutes.

The welfare of children is seen to depend not only on material benefits, close contact with both parents, role models of both sexes, and on a good educational milieu, but on a reunion of the child and adult worlds. This presupposes a society in which men and women share equally in childcare, voluntary work for the community, and gainful employment. All the efforts that have been made to achieve this more equal division of social responsibilities underline the need for changes in the organization and the goals of production and in the values society places on various types of activity. Can the next generation be educated to take the initiative?

Notes

1. *"I Want to Work But What About the Kids?"* (Manchester: Equal Opportunities Commission, 1978), p. 9.

2. Alfred J. Kahn and Sheila B. Kamerman, *Social Services in International Perspective* (Washington, D.C.: U.S. Department of Health, Education, and Welfare, 1977), p. 167.

3. Martin Woodhead, "Pre-School Provision in Western Europe" (Paper presented at the conference "From Birth to Eight: Young Children in European Society in the 1980s," Council for Europe, Strasbourg, December 17-20, 1979), p. 42.

4. *Day Care for Small Children: A Debate Report from the Family Aid Commission* (Stockholm: Liber Förlag, 1979), p. 13.

5. Bror Rexed, "The Children's World and Ours," *Current Sweden* 108 (1976).

6. Annika Baude, "Public Policy and Changing Family Patterns in Sweden, 1930–1977," in Jean Lipman-Blumen and Jessie Bernard, eds., *Sex Roles and Social Policy* (London and Beverly Hills: Sage Publications, 1979), p. 169.

7. English summary, report of the Nordic Cultural Commission's committee for the investigation of sex roles in education to the Nordic Council of Ministers, *Sex Roles and Education: A Report from the Nordic Council* (Stockholm, June 1972).

8. Bodil Rosengren, *Pre-School in Sweden* (Stockholm: The Swedish Institute, 1973), p. 21.

9. Camilla Odhnoff, "Equality is for Children Too," *Current Sweden* 98 (1975): 2.

10. Quoted in R. Misiti and L. Benigni, "The Fundamental Needs of the Young Child and Society's Answer to These Needs" (Paper presented at the conference "From Birth to Eight: Young Children in European Society in the 1980s," Council for Europe, Strasbourg, December 17-20, 1979), p. 11.

11. *Day Care for Small Children*, pp. 28-29.

12. William van der Eyken, Lynn Michell, and Jane Grubb, *Pre-Schooling in England, Scotland and Wales*: (Department of Child Health, University of Bristol, 1979), pp. 18 ff.

13. Eva Nordland, "Trends in European Society Which Affect the Upbringing of Young Children" (Paper presented at the conference "From Birth to Eight: Young Children in European Society in the 1980s," Council for Europe, Strasbourg, December 17-20, 1979), p. 20.

CHAPTER 7

Education for a Freer Choice

"The division of the labor market into male and female is strongly reflected in recruitment to the integrated upper secondary school. So far vocational guidance and the intensified debate on sex roles have not succeeded in breaking the traditional pattern of sex related study and career choice."[1]

Britta Stenholm
Chief Education Officer of
Täby near Stockholm

No institution has had so many and such rapidly changing and conflicting demands made upon it as the school, and the Swedish school is no exception. Since World War II, public education systems have been expected to counteract all manner of inequalities and give children the equal start in life they were not born with, to supply children with the skills currently needed by the economy while keeping young people off the labor market, to fit them to compete successfully in the world as it is but develop critical abilities that will enable them to change the world for the better. Moreover, it has been insisted that schools accomplish all this by treating children equally, at the same time giving special guidance to those who are unusually talented or appear to lag behind. Schools are to maintain close contact with real life, yet they must not be so career-oriented that they fail to develop well-rounded people with a solid grounding in their culture. The classroom should inculcate self-discipline, but not create an authoritarian atmosphere that will alienate and constrain young people. Pressure to perform must be relaxed (grades must be abolished); standards must be raised (grades must be restored). And so on.

As a reflection of societies' ever-shifting perspectives and priorities, the school systems in most countries are in an almost per-

petual state of reform, and this too is true for Sweden. But whatever the tasks at any given time, one thing remains constant. They
are left to the same group of people to carry out—the teaching
staff, usually women, usually poorly paid, and themselves the
product of the school system that has just been judged inadequate
(or the one that preceded it).

In the last few years education has been subjected to scrutiny
from a new angle, this time largely at the instigation of women.
The school has been seen as the institution that acts to perpetuate
and reinforce stereotyped roles which boys and girls have absorbed
in their families and in society from the moment they were born.
Although most state-supported school systems in industrialized
countries have for years been teaching girls and boys in the same
classes, offering them by and large the same subjects and officially
placing the same academic demands on them, what has been coming out is what went in. That is, young women emerge who "want
to work with people" and whose modest occupational goals are
secondary to what they see as their serious adult future—the creation of a home and family. Young men are graduated who want
to work with things, whose interests are mechanical, technological,
scientific and/or theoretical, and who know that a job comes first
and everything else comes afterwards. Card catalogues overflow
with references to literature explaining that the reason for this is
that this is the way it is. Girls are naturally quieter, want to please,
adapt to school, are good at routine tasks; boys are hard to manage, naturally aggressive, late bloomers, but logical thinkers, have a
spatial sense, will build the cities of tomorrow.

In the last fifteen years work in applied psychology, physi-
ology, biology, and anthropology has helped to dispel in the minds
of some educators the belief that boys and girls are born with gen-
der-related capacities that are sufficiently different and immutable
to account for two distinct streams of educational accomplish-
ment. Still more recently researchers have turned their attention
to the classroom itself and tried to find out what teachers do, in-
tentionally or unconsciously, that encourages dependence in girls
and aggressiveness in boys, and how this differentiated treatment
may influence girls' verbal skills and boys' ability to solve problems on their own.[2] "Dick and Jane" textbooks were the first and
most obvious targets. The small girl, learning to read, had before
her the housewife-mother as a model, with an occasional teacher

or shop assistant thrown in. Boys saw themselves from the beginning as pilots, doctors, automobile mechanics, frogmen, supermen.
We are now seeing the beginning of the next stage, in which schools themselves are considering how the educational system could be used to combat the effects of stereotyping and encourage children and young people to use their full human potential.[3]
When the call goes out for studies of programs designed to provide both sexes with the same chances for development, Swedish schools will offer an admirable locale for field work, for it appears that here too, Sweden (again in cooperation with other Scandinavian countries) has a head start of a decade or more.

The present Swedish nine-year comprehensive school was established in 1962. It begins in the year the child turns seven, and takes all pupils through a uniform course until they are 16. In the last three years (that is, beginning at age 14) an optional subject and two periods of "freely chosen work" are introduced, and children are separated by sex for physical education.

From the beginning the curriculum has included home economics and childcare for both boys and girls, but originally sewing was reserved for girls and metal- and woodworking for boys. This traditional division of handicrafts was strongly criticized by the Social Democratic Party's "study group on women's questions" which, in the 1964 "Erlander Report," also placed great stress on the need for vocational guidance to play a much more decisive role than hitherto in encouraging "a freer and less sex-dominated vocational choice." Girls must be encouraged, it said, "to seek new, male-dominated vocations and attempts should be made to dispel boys' resistance to nursing and other 'female' occupations." Anticipating changes in the secondary schools, which were then in the process of being reorganized into a unified system, the report called on parents, teachers, vocational-guidance officers, and employers to join forces so that "girls' aptitude for science and technical subjects" should not be wasted. A review of textbooks and a study of their effect on childrens' ideas about the roles of men and women in society was an essential condition for reform, it was asserted.[4]

The guidelines of the Swedish National Board of Education for the comprehensive school in 1969, and for the new "integrated upper secondary school" in 1970, were generous in their directives for combating the fixed attitudes that even young children bring to school with them, and for furthering "a free choice of study and career." The school was to stimulate pupils to question how and why existing differences in the treatment of the sexes arose, and how these differing expectations affected free choice and the status of the individual in society. These questions were to be examined not only in connection with the career-orientation program, but in the context of social-science, language, history, and religion courses. The students were to be made "aware that a prerequisite for equality between the spouses, on the labor market, and in society as a whole is the equal division of childcare and home chores between men and women in the family."[5] Since the introduction of the 1969 curriculum, beginning in 1970—71, girls and boys have had handwork both in textiles and in metal- and woodworking through the first six grades. Domestic science is compulsory for both sexes in the eighth and ninth grade, and in this last year the subjects include childcare. During the eighth grade each child pays a visit to three different types of workplace, and in the ninth has a period of practice at an actual job. In the last three years, pupils choose an optional course in a technical subject, a foreign language, economics, or the arts, and may select whether they want to continue in textile handicrafts, or metal- and woodworking.

Graduation from the ninth class automatically qualifies the pupil for the integrated secondary school. Established in 1971, this school combined the diverse vocational, professional, and pre-university schools into one system, as part of the general democratization of education. It does away with the division between purely vocational and academic training by offering a choice of three lines—scientific and technical, economic, and the humanities—with a total of some 20 course combinations that may last two, three, or four years. Almost all of these combinations now qualify graduates for higher education.

Hardly had this major school reorganization been launched when the National Board of Education undertook a "Sex-Role Project" to determine what measures could be used to intensify the influence of the school toward a less traditional choice of subjects by sex, and ultimately to a freer selection of further education and employment. This five-year research project was described by its director, Margareta Vestin, in a talk to the Nordic Cultural Commission symposium in 1971. She defined the goal as

> Increased clarity regarding what knowledge we must have in dealing with education and teaching; what must be included in curriculum plans and instructional materials; what areas require methodology planning; what should happen to the pupil and teacher environment of the school; what is required in the way of possible changes in scheduling and school structure; and what can be done with the study and career guidance programs.[6]

One aspect of the Sex-Role Project was a review of Swedish and foreign literature on role learning and sex-role differentiation. In addition, various subprojects were set up. The content and teaching of the Swedish language and physics were examined. Individual schools tried out various combinations of new teaching approaches and strengthened vocational guidance. Attitudes of teachers, parents, and pupils were surveyed, and various models of in-service training for teachers on sex-role questions were tried out. A study package for parents' organizations was also produced and evaluated.

In a typical Swedish comprehensive school serving a working-class district in Stockholm, where most of the parents were employed in a factory making communications equipment, intensive cooperation had been developed in the early seventies between the full-time vocational guidance officer, Eva Johannesson, a sympathetic woman in her late fifties, and the social-science teacher, Marta Fröman, a younger woman, full of energy and ideas. Both were militant supporters of sex-role equality and anxious to see the school play a positive role in changing attitudes.

In 1975, the year the Board of Education's Sex-Role Project ended, Marta Fröman was using TV cassettes in her social-science class (reputedly the toughest in the school) for a discussion of sex roles that had a concrete bearing on her pupils' lives. Almost all the problems presented for their analysis in these TV enactments involved teenage girls in conflict between their sexuality and their fantasy images of themselves as glamor girls or secure housewives, and their struggling realization that what in fact awaited them was a trap. In one TV playlet a sixteen-year-old girl was offered a job as a "photographers' model." All she had to do was pay for the "training." In another, a girl was shown in violent clash with her older sister who lived only for her semidetached house. In a third, a young girl announced to her mother that she was pregnant, that she intended to have the baby, and that she expected her mother would take care of it while she finished school and got a job. Her mother refused, having just got a job herself after many years at home.

The girls in the class, already tall and physically developed, were not very articulate but they were drawn into a debate through the joint efforts of the social-science teacher and the vocational-guidance officer, who was also present. They agreed in the case of the pregnant schoolgirl, for example, that her mother was right to refuse to care for the baby. Now she was in a tough spot. She'd have to take the first job that came along. Later she'd be unhappy and think about what she might have done with her life. The boys, still small and skinny, sat silent. Then one of them pointed out that the father in the case would have to pay child support for 18 years.

These pupils had also seen and discussed the play *Knocked Up and Cracked Up* (referred to in Chapter 5) performed by one of the traveling theatre companies commissioned by the Board of Health and Welfare. Marta Fröman was startled by the language, but her pupils advised her to come along to the discotheque and find out how kids really talk. Some of her own students had written, in more socially acceptable language, a humorous review called *Male and Female* and had performed it for several school assemblies under Marta's direction. In one typical scene, a teenage school-leaver was auctioned off to the highest bidder:

The auctioneer: 'Well gentlemen, here's Susanne. Her vital statistics are 91-51-98. Paws off, gentlemen. Take a look at this merchandise—sorry —girl. She's a bargain. She has finished elementary school—she is a beauty—she doesn't know what she wants to be. She would like a glamorous profession, but you know, gentlemen, they are hard to find. She can come and go as you please. She lives with Mother. When she gets married she'll settle in the suburbs. When she has children she'll quit work. When production rises you can call her. In short, gentlemen, she's a splendid labor reserve. Is there any low-wage enterprise, textiles perhaps, that is interested? She has excellent eyesight. Seven crowns an hour. This girl always takes it, mostly she says nothing. Do I hear nine crowns? Going . . . going . . ."

Susanne: "Enough!"

Marta kept the subject alive in her class. When the girls asked her what to do she told them, "Education and more Education. Only then will you be in a position to change society yourself, and only then will people listen to you."

Eva Johannesson, the vocational-guidance officer, talked to the girls and their parents. She held her consultations at an hour convenient for fathers, using material being tested by the Board of Education. She discussed women's double role and a fairer division of tasks in the family. The fathers were embarrassed for themselves, but they did want a better life for their daughters. They were convinced by statistics that most women will have to support themselves at one time or another, and that marriage is not a career. Still, they didn't want to see their little girls "get their hands dirty."

Eva defined her work as "getting the girls to change their minds." She found them at sixteen more conservative than their parents.

> When I ask them what they want to do, better than 99 percent want to be telephone operators, nurses, dressmakers, or secretaries. Or go into childcare. When one of them tells me she wants to be a nurse, I remind her that the work is tough, the pay is bad, the hours long. If she is good in science I tell her that she is one of those who could have the best education in Sweden, that she could be a doctor or a dentist, that she has a responsibility to help show the way. I tell her I'm going to nag her till she does something about it.

Sometimes a girl will confess that she secretly wants to be a doctor but is afraid to say so for fear the class will laugh at her.

> But except for the girls with really good marks we are only marking time. If she has poor marks I have to find an education she can manage, which is usually in a caretaking service.

According to Johannesson, this school had a sympathetic headmaster and "the best school doctor in Stockholm" who could give a spellbinding talk on contraception. But many of the teachers were indifferent to the sex-role debate, and discussion with the younger children had not begun yet. The two weeks' vocational practice in the ninth grade was largely a formality because, while theoretically the pupils could chose what they wanted to try, in practice the school had to send them to the places that were available.

Had there been no change?

> Yes, there has been. *Every* girl now thinks in terms of a job. This *is* progress. They want children, but they don't pin their hopes on marriage. They don't intend to be housewives for some future husband. But there has been no change in their vocational choices.

This was the central lesson that emerged in the 800-page report that resulted from the Sex-Role Project, which was subsequently reduced to a 250-page manual for teachers called *A Freer Choice*. In the words of Margareta Vestin:

> We have found out that there is no correlation between giving instruction and the final choice of a vocation. We have had model schools where they have given a lot of sex-role instruction and had coeducational gymnastics and so on, and there is no difference at all—in attitudes, of course, but in their choices, no.

The major proposals put forward in the report she presented in 1975 were the following.

The curriculum should be altered so that every girl and every boy will have to try fields where their sex is at present in the minority. Technology and economics should be compulsory instead of optional in grades 7—9. Physical education should be coeducational throughout the elementary school; handicrafts and shop should be given to girls and boys alike at the upper level, and more hours should be devoted to childcare. There should be compensatory training for boys who have less experience with children and for girls who need practice in manipulating tools, not under the heading of "sex-role problems" but on an individual basis.

The climate in teaching science and technology has to be altered. The Swedish investigations confirmed other findings that boys who had been trained from their earliest years to use their

spatial sense and the language that goes with it could understand
proofs given in visual form better than girls, while girls understood
verbal explanations better than boys. Also, in the words of Vestin:

> The whole climate in the sciences is very masculine. Very tough and
> competitive. Girls who aren't personally very strong fail. We have inter-
> views showing that some girls feel discriminated against by their teach-
> ers and male comrades even if they are not. Another thing is that boys
> who begin physics with bad marks may come out with good ones, but
> this doesn't happen with girls. We think it is because boys feel they
> need physics for their future and that society expects them to do well,
> while girls do not. We think, too, that physics requires the self-confi-
> dence to ask special kinds of questions, and that boys are socialized to
> be more self-assured. We want more laboratory work to be available for
> girls who need it.[7]

*The school environment, which is itself a mirror of the situ-
ation in society, must be changed.* Ninety percent of school prin-
cipals are men; 99 percent of teachers at the lower level are
women. The canteen is run by women. There should be more male
teachers for the primary-school pupils, more women among teachers at the senior level. According to Vestin:

> We think there should be a change in the decision-making system in the
> schools, a sort of laymen's board making a lot of the decisions, and
> also some kind of a standing committee connecting school and work-
> ing life. The membership in all these boards and committees and confer-
> ences should be divided between women and men, 50—50. If we don't
> say this specifically, they'll have all the old boys there. This is also a
> very important point when training girls for leadership, because if we
> have the old model of decision making with the boss at the top there
> will be very few females asking for those jobs. Women don't like being
> tough like that. Of course, we could also train the males to be a little
> more female.

Vocational guidance should be intensified. It should start
with field trips and discussions in the first year of the comprehensive school. A vocational practice period in a nontraditional field
should be compulsory for both sexes, and it should be arranged on
an individual basis.

In addition, teaching materials should be subject to continuous scrutiny, and there should be closer cooperation between the

school, the parents, and the community to ensure that what is taught in school is not undone but reinforced by pupils' experience outside it.

In connection with the project, a list of teaching aids and an outline of sex-role instruction for the entire period of comprehensive— and secondary-school education was drawn up. A four-year program for teacher in-service training and study groups was suggested which was expected to lead educators to examine their own attitudes and make them conscious of whether they really treated girls and boys the same way and had the same expectations of them. The report proposed a documentation service at the National Board of Education to advise teachers where to find material for vocational guidance and discussion, and a handbook with supplements to be issued every six months.

The Sex-Role Project report was circulated to various agencies for suggestions, and in 1978 was transformed into an equality program for schools which included a revision of the comprehensive-school curriculum. Before the government could propose legislation on the basis of this program, however, yet another reorganization of the elementary-school system took effect in 1978. This plan, known as SIA (for "the inner work of the school") placed more responsibility on the school for the all-around development of pupils by incorporating more free activities into a longer school day, and by introducing a much more intensive vocational orientation. The responsibility for the comprehensive school has from the beginning been in the hands of elected municipal school committees, but SIA gave the local authorities greater powers to make decisions in school matters. A far-reaching study and vocational-orientation program was launched, with the goal of a full-time study and vocational counselor for each 750 pupils. Their job, in addition to personal counseling, is to see that students have a clear idea of the world of work that awaits them, its organization, the work environment, the division of labor, and employer-employee relations. Participation in teaching by people with practical work experience, including representatives of labor and management and the employment services, is supposed to intensify the contact of the school with the realities of working life. According to still more recent changes, six to ten weeks of practical work experience are to be arranged for each pupil in the course of the nine-year comprehensive school. This should be divided along three lines: technology and manufacturing, commerce and agriculture, office work and services. In the secondary school each student will spend a week at a practical job in each academic year.

Local planning councils are being set up in each municipality to make a more practical orientation of the school toward working life possible, involving representatives of the school, the employment service, and employer and labor organizations. They will, for example, arrange and coordinate the schools' requirements for study visits and jobs, and arrange for the training of instructors for these activities.

One of the main purposes of this reform was to combat youth unemployment and the educational failures that appear to have contributed to it. This in itself has an equality dimension, since it is girls between 16 and 19 who are most likely to discontinue their education and have the greatest trouble finding jobs. The changes theoretically offer possibilities for intensifed effort to discuss segregation on the labor market and combat it, but it is too early to see any results. The reorganization of the school day and the emphasis upon vocational orientation place so many new demands on the teaching staff and the school administration, whose members for the most part are not trained in leading leisure-time activities or in handling vocational and labor-market questions, that in practice sex-role questions do not appear to be receiving increased attention.

The decentralization of decision making, which is being heavily stressed in all aspects of Swedish life today, weakens the ability of the Board of Education to exert direct pressure. Since 1979 the Board has no sex-role projects of its own, and impulses no longer come from the center. It is up to the regional education authorities to analyze their specific situation and draw up a program. The board will continue to direct an information campaign at municipalities and teachers based on favorable experiences of individual schools or school personnel, and reviewing new literature.

"One thing we know," a representative of the Board of Education declared in 1979, "is that the municipalities haven't done very much because they are concentrating on employment for young people." The Committee on Equality between Men and

Women has been sharply critical, saying, "All the measures taken so far are mere drops in the ocean." Training in the presentation of sex-role issues, it points out, is not yet part of the teacher's basic education, and so can only be added afterwards during the limited number of days available annually for in-service training, which must be shared with numerous other issues. Textbooks are scrutinized, but not sufficiently strictly, it charges: "Educational staff, like everybody else, are bogged down in a routine sex-role approach."[8]

As things stand today, there has been no appreciable change since the beginning of the seventies in the study choices made by girls and boys at the secondary school level (Table 8). Between 1971 and 1978 the share of girls in secondary-school education rose from 46 percent to 49 percent, and this was reflected in a greater concentration of women in predominantly female lines. Two of the three secondary-school subject divisions are almost completely dominated by one sex. Girls are only 3 percent of the total in technical and scientific courses; boys are 6 percent in the arts and social sciences. The economics and commercial line is 55 percent female. There has been a slight increase in the percent of girls studying in the four-year technical line, from 7 percent in 1971 to 11 percent in 1978.

Among the approximately 20 percent of young people who reach the universities, however, some signs of change are apparent. The proportion of women in higher education rose by 7 percent during the seventies, and 38 percent of new students in 1978 were female. Women's share in almost all the major branches has risen (Table 9). In 1978 women were on their way to 40 percent of students in medicine, and were more than one-third of all those in mathematics and the natural sciences. The increase in those studying technology was very slight, from 12 percent in 1973 to 14 percent, but the figure in 1969 had been only 6 percent.

It has been argued that the age at which girls and boys make their educational choices, and thus for the most part their vocational decisions, is a particularly unfortunate one from the point of view of a better balance between the sexes. This is the period when young people are most anxious about establishing their identity as feminine or masculine and least likely to make choices that seem inconsistent with that image. Such a perspective has been incorporated in Swedish labor-market philosophy. The National Labor Market Board's "Equality Program" adopted in 1977 argues:

> Sex roles are most manifest and sensitive between the ages of 14 and
> 25, which is the stage when a person finds it necessary to prove his or
> her essential capability as a man or woman. Only when this identity has
> been successfully established does one feel ready to go on and become
> a whole person. This thesis is supported by the strongly traditional ed-
> ucational choices of young people and by investigations which show that
> it is in the middle aged families that patterns of equality are best incul-
> cated.[9]

The recent trend toward a somewhat wider range of choices by
women at the university level does not upset this hypothesis. In
Sweden, as in other countries, children's educational choices have
been found to be heavily influenced by the educational level in the
family. In Sweden in 1972, 80 percent of boys and 65 percent of
girls from families where one or both parents had a higher education chose three- or four-year study lines in the secondary school
that could lead to the university, while this was true for only 12
percent of girls and boys from the families of unskilled workers.
Among university students, women and men coming from homes
with a higher-educational background are almost equally represented, while women are heavily underrepresented among students
from the working class, who in turn are underrepresented in the
university population. Since women brought up in families where
higher education is the rule are more likely than the average to
make "unconventional" choices, it is not surprising that the figures for university choices are more promising than those for the
secondary school. It would be overoptimistic to attribute this shift
primarily to sex-role instruction in the lower grades, although it
certainly reflects the general change in atmosphere regarding
women's roles.

Some encouragement for the belief that the stimulus for self-
realization that girls are now receiving in school has a latent effect
is found in the fact that at all levels of adult education more
women participate than men, and that polls show women more interested than men in further education. Such a conclusion underlies the value of repeated opportunites for further education and
retraining throughout adult life; this is also an aspect of the Swedish
effort to open out the school toward the community. The expansion of labor-market training and recent school reforms point in

this direction, as does a decision by parliament that will lead to a restructuring of university-level study, making it available to new categories of students including skilled workers, and establishing branch campuses of Sweden's six universities in an additional eleven locations.

Proposals that are currently being studied by the government to strengthen the drive for greater equality in education include the idea of giving special academic credits to boys and girls making nontraditional choices in the secondary school. Ways of recruiting more women to top jobs in the school system are being considered. The National Board of Education itself, as a government agency, is affected by the government directive of 1976 (described in Chapter 2), calling on central agencies to adopt plans for advancing women. Thought is also being given to introducing quotas favoring the underrepresented sex in certain branches of higher education. Funds have been obtained for more equality research, and a number of universities have projects under way.

Several small projects are being run by the Committee on Equality. One aims to show the new municipal committees for co-operation between the schools and working life how they can influence boys and girls in their choices. Others involve experiments with teacher in-service training and teaching aids. A pilot project launched by the committee in 1979 focuses on the middle level of one average comprehensive school, where all resources will be focused on the age group 10—12. Equality will be part of all instruction, special training will be given to the teachers, new teaching materials will be tried out. Boys and girls will learn to cook, clean, and make household repairs, and will be given special opportunities to try out different occupations. Parents who themselves have made unconventional job choices will be called on to cooperate.

It doesn't escape the educational reformers, naturally, that one of the greatest obstacles standing in the way of a freer choice for boys and girls, women and men, in education is the situation on the labor market as well as the division of responsibilities in the home which it helps to perpetuate. Baude has commented:

> I believe that one of the reasons why the various school reforms have not yet had a greater impact on study and career choices among girls is the fact that girls receive a two-sided message during their school years

.... The whole school environment is informed by an attitude of
equality between the sexes. But the reality outside the school is something quite different. And this must make a satisfactory adjustment to
that reality very difficult, particularly since there is little discussion in
the school about how to combine work with childcare.[10]

If the job market is shrinking, except in the caretaking services, what reason is there to expect a girl to choose a technical
line of study? Although employers and labor-market officials have
repeatedly stated that there is a field for women who choose to be
skilled workers and technicians, firms are not reserving places for
such women nor are they asking the employment service to train
women for jobs that will be available a year or two hence. The
Equality Committee was shocked to discover that, when a local
shortage of labor developed in central Sweden in the late 1970s,
certain industries imported male workers from the north rather
than making use of the Labor Market Board's elaborate vocational
program to train local unemployed women. Moreover, the schools
will probably soon have to alert girls to the fact that their traditional job area, the tertiary sphere, is being invaded by men as part
of the sex-role equality drive, and that it behooves them to prepare for the competition if this sector is not to reproduce the
stratification pattern of the labor market as a whole.

In the long term, these contradictions must emerge from the
education children are getting in sex-role equality. When a new
fifth-grade mathematics textbook, for example, teaches percentages
on the basis of the distribution of women and men in employment
and in decision-making posts in Sweden, and asks the pupils to discuss the reasons for this situation, it can be said that these children
are being educated to bring about change. Is this to become a goal
of the school, or simply a by-product? Margareta Vestin raised the
problem a decade ago in her lecture to the Nordic Cultural Commission:

The most difficult question concerning equality is, in my opinion: what
values are we to embrace? Is it our aim to "get women out" on the labor market and into the political life with the unchanged goals of increasing the GNP, advancing our technological standards, and encouraging consumption of even more merchandise per individual? Or should
we, in our discussion with the students, tell them how things are in reality—that there are divergent opinions on this point. Our country has

no one predominant idea about what is a happy development for our society and others. Concretely, this means: are we to encourage girls to go for a career at any price—as if they were men? To enter the commercially and technically "heavy" professions to the same degree as men in order to thereby gain a place in "heavy" decision-making situations? Or should we try to make the boys sacrifice their careers? Encourage them not to care about exercising power? To consider the care of groups of children and old people as at least as important for human happiness as increased technological progress?[11]

This "most difficult question" cannot, of course, be answered for the school system alone. It expresses an ambiguity that is built into the whole drive for sex-role equality.

Notes

1. Britta Stenholm, "Upper Secondary Education in Sweden," *Current Sweden* 137 (1976): 7.

2. See, for example, Katherine Clarricoates, " 'Dinosaurs in the Classroom': A Re-examination of Some Aspects of the 'Hidden' Curriculum in the Primary Schools," *Women's Studies International Quarterly* 1, no. 4 (1978): 353-64.

3. As the organizers of a conference on "Sex Differentiation and Schooling" held at Cambridge University in England in January 1980 declared in their announcement: "Despite recent legislation on both sides of the Atlantic, and the work of the Equal Opportunities Commission, many people are worried that schools are working through sex stereotypes, and thus being fair to neither girls nor boys. This conference will be an important and unique opportunity to work towards change."

4. *Women's Equality: A Programme for the Future*, report of the Social Democratic Party study group on women's questions (Stockholm, photocopy, no date), pp. 27-34.

5. Quoted in Margareta Vestin, "School, Instruction, and Sex Role Questions" (Lecture delivered at the Nordic Cultural Commission Symposium, October 1971 in Copenhagen, National Swedish Board of Education), p. 4.

6. Ibid., p. 16.

7. Using data from an international achievement survey conducted in 1973, Alison Kelly and Helen Weinreich-Haste ("Science is for Girls," *Women's Studies International Quarterly* 2, no. 3 (1979): 275-94) show that while the difference in achievement between boys and girls remains relatively constant from country to country, girls in a few countries have higher mean scores than boys in others. Thus Japanese girls score higher than boys in Sweden, the United States, England, and France but not in Germany; Hungar-

ian girls score ahead of boys in Belgium and on a level with boys in England. For a discussion of why girls do not do as well as boys in science and how science teaching might be altered, see Anne Fausto-Sterling, "Women and Science," *Women's Studies International Quarterly*, 1981 (in press).

8. "Report from the Swedish Government to the ECE seminar on the participation of women in the economic evolution of the ECE region" (Stockholm, March 1979), p. 24.

9. "Equality in the Labour Market: Program Adopted by the Labour Market Board" (Solna: National Labour Market Board, September 1977), p. 7.

10. Annika Baude, "Public Policy and Changing Family Patterns in Sweden," in Jean Lipman-Blumen and Jessie Bernard, eds., *Sex Roles and Social Policy* (London and Beverly Hills: Sage Publications, 1979), p. 165.

11. Vestin, "School, Instruction, and Sex Role Questions," p. 12.

CHAPTER 8

The Man-Made Environment

How will women and men live together in the future? Radical changes in the relationships between people require radical changes in life-styles, and thus in the way people arrange their physical dwellings.

Although sometimes inspired by socialist sympathies, the low-cost housing built in Western Europe between the two world wars did not have as its goal the remodeling of the family or society, but of ameliorating one of the ugliest by-products of capitalism—the squalid slum life of the industrial cities. The goals were space, hygiene, and fresh air. The model was what the bourgeoisie was enjoying, adapted, of course, to a much more modest scale. Thus the garden cities of England and the blocks of workers' flats on the continent built in the 1920s and 1930s were designed for the full-time housewife, even though many working-class women were employed and needed to be relieved of household drudgery. This impractical pattern of living has been duplicated on a bigger and better scale all over the industrialized world, including the Soviet Union, since World War II. Although women rarely had a voice in the design of the dwelling they were to inhabit, when they did they seemed mesmerized by the kitchen as a status symbol and the idea that a private collection of gadgets would ultimately shorten the time spent in housework. Meanwhile the total hours spent by women in unpaid work approached the number of hours put in by the paid work force, and it has remained there.[1]

Sweden, because of its late urbanization, never suffered the kind of industrial slums that grew up around the early industrial centers. Nevertheless, the Social Democratic government did develop a social policy on housing in the 1930s to which it could refer when a wave of population migration toward the major cities and larger towns began after World War II. The aim in the mid-thirties was to rehouse the 20,000 urban families with three or more children in which more than two persons occupied a single room. The houses were to have open space between them, access to a playground, and a playgroup or cooperative nursery was considered desirable. Two points worth noting are that the parents did not have to be married to be eligible, and that subsidies, instead of being paid on building costs, were given directly to the tenants to reduce the rent. Only 6,000 of these units were constructed before the outbreak of the war placed other demands on the economy.

Whereas in 1940 only 56 percent of the Swedish population lived in "urban localities" of 200 inhabitants or more, by 1960 the figure was 73 percent and by 1970, 81 percent. This population shift was accompanied by the demand for better housing standards, and the result was an acute housing shortage requiring young couples to wait many years before they could move into a place of their own. Through laws passed in the 1940s, parliament was made the responsible agent for the country's overall housing plan, while the municipalities were given the obligation and the authority to draw up and see to the execution of local building programs and to exercise rent control. Most local authorities started buying up land destined for development in the early sixties, and when the Social Democratic government decided to solve the shortage by constructing one million dwelling units between 1965 and 1974, the municipalities were in a position to exercise strict control over construction, whether they leased their property to private or public firms. State loans at low interest with long amortization periods favored cooperative and municipal building companies, and in the early seventies these accounted for 60—65 percent of new units produced.

The state-supported housing program achieved an annual building rate twice the average for the European members of the Organization for Economic Cooperation and Development, and public control made possible highly coordinated planning for urban expansion. Sweden rejected both the British "new town" concept of independent self-contained communities built from scratch, and the spontaneous process of agglomeration and suburban sprawl typical for the United States. It adopted instead the idea of satellite communities connected with the old urban center by public transport, but supplying its residents with adequate services and entertainment and, ideally, a certain number of job opportunities, locally. Stockholm represents the ultimate in this type of urban planning. The master plan for Stockholm drawn up in the forties and fifties called for urban districts strung out along the subway system, which was simultaneously extended in five directions from the center of the city. These individual centers each serve several thousand people, housed in multiple-dwelling buildings varying from three to ten or more floors, interspersed with groups of one-family houses. Each of these developments has a subway station, a school, day-care centers, a playground, and local shops within easy walking distance. Several of these communities comprise a group which has a larger shopping center, entertainment facilities, and social services, usually five minutes away by car or bus. None are more than half an hour from the center of Stockholm by public transport. Green belts separate these mini-cities, and traffic is completely separate from pedestrian and bicycle ways which continue outward into parks and recreation areas. The size of flats and the level of amenities has steadily improved. While in the units opened in the fifties 60 percent of flats had two rooms plus kitchen or less, in those finished in the early seventies 50 percent had three rooms plus kitchen and another 20 percent were larger.

Thanks to public control, to Sweden's generally high level of planning and design, and to the low density of the population which ensures relatively easy access to the countryside for all city dwellers, these satellite towns compare favorably with any of the vast expanses of multiple-unit dwellings which surround most of the big cities of Europe. The Swedes, however, are not urbanites but for the most part only first- or second-generation city dwellers, and even young people find cities a hostile climate. In the experience of Gösta Carlestam and Lennart Levi, two Swedish authorities on urban environment and stress,

> Various reactions of dissatisfaction and annoyance or even disease may be provoked even in the presence of environmental conditions that would be characterized by the majority of a population as being most favorable and pleasant.[2]

Thresholds of alienation differ widely. What would be bearable in Rome is unbearable in Stockholm.

Whereas the dwellings planned in the fifties and early sixties seemed to meet the demand of the affluent society for bigger apartments and more and bigger shopping malls, by the mid-sixties, as one observer put it, the affluent society had become the querulous society. Criticism erupted over the Skarholmen group in Stockholm, comprising four satellite communities, the first of which was ready in 1963. In Skarholmen the planners thought they had achieved the ultimate in town planning. They boasted that they had provided tens of thousands of square metres of shopping areas, office space, multi-level parking, and many other such attractions, serving 37,000 people in 11,700 dwelling units of which 86 percent were in multi-family houses ranging from three to eight stories. The Skarholmen group had 24 elementary schools, more than 2,000 day-care places, and 10 playgrounds with supervisory personnel. It was only 23 minutes to the center of Stockholm on the subway.

By the time the shopping mall opened in 1968, public criticism of this man-made environment had reached a peak. "Pull down Skarholmen!" the daily *Dagens Nyheter* cried. It serves the function "car driver" and the function "consumer," the paper charged, but there is no place for the human being. We need a place where humans will want to meet even when they are not on their way to buy furniture or beer. What was being inaugurated, the reporter said, was the slums of the seventies, and those present at the ceremony saw ahead to the cold winter evenings when the wind would blow between the cliffs, the shops would be closed, and there would be nothing to do but clang beer bottles.

Criticism was not directed only at the stereotyped appearance of the concrete cliffs, the monotony of the urban landscape, and the high density of the population. The disenchanted residents charged that, while shops and commercial services were quick to appear in these centers, nurseries, social services, play opportunities, and places where adults could get together and do things without spending money came much later and sometimes never. Some 60 percent of Stockholm's population now lived outside the city center, but only 28 percent of job opportunities were there, and this was a particular bone of contention for the many women who were entering or reentering the labor market.

One answer to this criticism came from a government committee on services headed by the then minister of Family Affairs,

Camilla Odhnoff. Its establishment coincided with the beginning
of the emphasis on sex-role equality, and the impetus for its for-
mation was the acute need for day care and for services for the
elderly and the handicapped now that so many women were working. The committee worked from 1967 to 1973, and its numerous
reports helped to create support for services directed at people's
needs rather than profits. There was a demand for facilities that
would help to break down the anonymity and isolation of individuals to give people places and occasions for meeting outside the
family. The principle was established that when builders obtained
construction loans for housing they could at the same time borrow
the money to develop such service arrangements.

The first housing estate built with this kind of a service area
was Brickebacken in Örebro, a county in central Sweden with
some 120,000 inhabitants, a diversified economy, and about one-
third of the working population employed in manufacturing. The
county had an exceptionally forward-looking building program, initiated by its own nonprofit housing corporation. This, by the end
of the 1960s, had built ten housing areas for 40,000 people, giving
special attention to noncommercial services for children and adults.
It was on the basis of this experience that Brickebacken was
planned, and thanks to the government service committee it was
able to get funding for its unconventional arrangements.

The aim was a housing area that would attract different kinds
of people. According to Karin Kallin, who, at the time Brickebacken
was built, was one of the leading Social Democratic politicians in
Örebro and head of the department for the social aspects of housing in the Örebro council:

> When we planned Brickebacken we asked ourselves how we could use
> the earlier traditional services for the needs of new groups, how we
> could make it easier for both parents to take a job, how we could bring
> various age groups together, and how we could solve the two most im-
> portant problems for the aged which formerly made them seek institu-
> tional care: security and contact with others.

Brickebacken, two and a half miles outside the city of Örebro,
accommodates 5,000 people in some 1,900 flats—about 500 of
them in six-story buildings, the rest in two-story units. The units
are separated by green space with playgrounds for small children
and day-care centers located on the way to the public transit sys-

tem. All the units are connected with the shopping and service center by covered footpaths. There are several groups of service flats for the elderly, consisting of one or two rooms and a kitchen and equipped with a signal system in every room to call the nurse on duty. These tenants may either cook for themselves or have their meals delivered to their rooms, and there are three sitting rooms for common use. Apartments for the elderly are assigned by the social-service department of the county on a doctor's recommendation.

Integration of the common areas of Brickebracken and versatility in their use were achieved by coordination between social-service departments in the planning stage. Kallin recalls that

> In earlier projects every department in the county council planned its special needs for the groups for which it was responsible. For Brickebacken all these departments were called together, met frequently, and arrived at a complex aim for overall planning for the first time. We also involved the commercial services in working for the same goal. The school workshops are used during the day by the children, in the evening they may be used by anyone. The restaurant serves school dinners and noon meals for those employed in the area, and is used by the tenants in the evenings. It can also be turned into a meeting room or taken over for family parties. The kitchen supplies the mobile meals for the elderly in the service flats. We thought it a good idea to have the school located in the service center so that children would have contact with other age groups. The service center isn't famous for its looks but because it was the first one in Sweden to try this complex integration.

The library serves the school as well as the other tenants, and has an adjoining sitting room with magazines and television, a coffee bar, and a fairy-tale room for children. The center also houses the children's clinic and the dental service.

The "service houses" built in Sweden since the wave of complaints incorporate facilities for informal and group activities. The complexes of buildings are smaller and no more high-rise structures are included, so there are more built-in opportunities for informal contacts. Planning is closely watched by the media, and several environmental action groups are pressing for the preservation of more of the natural and built environment and fewer concessions to the automobile. Tenants' groups, dormant during the sixties, now demand to be informed and consulted and have ac-

quired some additional rights. A service house needs personnel—
youth leaders, sports and hobby instructors, playground supervisors,
and social workers, as well as a joint tenants-staff committee, and
is likely to be as good as the efforts of all these people. The body
that succeeded the government's services committee, the Council
for Children's Play (see Chapter 6) has contributed to improving
and revitalizing existing housing estates and involving tenants in
this activity.

Margaret Mead, in an essay published in 1977 entitled "New
Towns to Set New Life Styles," outlined what she saw as the needs
a housing development must meet.³ She identified feelings of
community, continuity, and participation as essential to a successful neighborhood. This requires housing suitable for three generations, where young people can grow up, adults can work, and
the elderly can live out their lives in security; where families and
single individuals can live side by side. There must be services that
permit people to function in this way, and adequate job opportunities nearby. Women's need to have a place equal to that of
men must be met by the availability of group childcare, houses
that do not demand constant attention, and services that can be
obtained locally. Finally, it must be possible for all residents to be
able to participate in running their own community.

These conditions are met to a considerable degree by the best
of the service houses now existing in Sweden. Nevertheless, they
do not answer other needs many Swedes feel—for more privacy,
more quiet, and a greater closeness to nature. The long-term planners reckoned without the automobile. In the forties, when there
was one car for every 20 inhabitants of Stockholm, it was assumed
that most people wanted to live close to the public transport system and that very few wanted a home of their own. When young
couples were polled in the 1950s, only 30–40 percent said they
would prefer single-family houses to a flat in an apartment house.
By 1974, however, Sweden stood in first place in Europe in car
ownership, with a passenger automobile for every three people.

The planners also reckoned without the combined interaction
of tax policies and rent subsidies. During the sixties particularly,
the rise in the cost of building had led to substantial rent increases,
even though rents are fixed on the basis of cost prices, with municipally owned dwellings the standard. Because it was part of the
Social Democratic equality policy that families with a low income

or with several children should have the same access to good housing as those in a better financial situation, rent subsidies were introduced in 1969. Lower-income families were thus enabled to meet the higher rents, while those that did not qualify found it more advantageous to buy a home of their own. Under Sweden's highly progressive income-tax system, wage increases to meet inflation had catapulted them into a tax bracket where they had to pay not only an income tax of 50 percent but a 70 percent tax on marginal income. Since interest on loans is tax deductible and the value of homes is rising, investment in a house represented a tax break and a hedge against inflation for many middle-income families.

As more affluent tenants moved out of the early high-rise apartments, lower-income tenants moved in, increasing the percentage of families with social handicaps of various kinds. Vandalism and burglary of garages and storage bins grew, and teenagers with nowhere to go congregated in the common areas. This in turn provided further incentives for residents to move out. Demand has made a complete somersault in a decade. Whereas in the 1960s, 70 percent of the dwelling units built were in apartment houses (about double the percent in Norway and Denmark, where small-house building dominated from the beginning of the postwar period), in the 1970s, 70 percent of construction was devoted to owner-occupied homes. The newest high-rise suburbs had up to 20 percent of flats going begging, and in some localities the construction of dwellings for rent had ceased entirely.

Residents of the spreading areas of one- and two-family houses and row houses say they find more community spirit there than in the new satellite towns, more individual responsibility; and they are willing to put up with the greater inaccessibility of schools and services and the longer travel to work with greater dependence on the car. This trend, which perpetuates a family pattern based on the conventional division of labor, will be difficult to reverse. Proposals to limit the advantages home owners enjoy are not likely to meet with success in the present political climate. The "nonsocialist" coalition is pledged to protect home ownership. Private builders encourage demand, since they earn higher profits from the construction of individual dwellings than from standard blocks of flats. The growing community of home owners (now about half the adult population, still a low figure by European standards) naturally increases the pressure for benefits for those who choose to buy. Even the Social Democratic Party is divided on the subject (as the better-off workers buy homes). One section finds home owners a privileged group with a vested interest in private property whose existence is inconsistent with the aims of the socialist labor movement, and is alarmed by the increasing social segregation of neighborhoods. The other considers it quite natural for workers to enjoy the benefits the welfare state has made available. Only the small Communist Party takes an unequivocal position against private homes.

Sweden's seemingly irreversible movement into single-family, owner-occupied dwellings may, however, come up against yet another trend. Today the energy crisis and strong feeling in Sweden against nuclear power (even though the country is more dependent on nuclear energy than almost any other) would seem to make modification of the present style of life inevitable, thus opening the way to new proposals. Two minority solutions have in fact begun to attract interest, at least from those who are seriously concerned with developing alternative life styles that would meet the twin requirements of energy saving and equality between the sexes. These are communes and collective houses.

Most modern proposals for the planned alteration of family life trace their ancestry back directly or indirectly to the utopian socialists of the nineteenth century. Charles Fourier and Etienne Cabet in France, Robert Owen in England, and others of that era attempted to salvage the equality and fraternity promised by the French Revolution by designing societies that would cure the already evident evils of capitalism through the application of Reason. The members of these utopian colonies would make a clean break with surrounding society, and eliminate from their community and their private lives all forms of inequality and exploitation. Numerous experimental settlements were founded to realize these visions, most of them in the United States, where land was plentiful and the mentality of Protestant dissent encouraged ethical radicalism.

The aim was to break the bonds that private property and conventional family ties imposed on the development of the individual in a free society. In these communities, property was owned jointly, work was shared, food was prepared in common, and children were brought up together. Every commune had, or aimed to have, its own school, community center, school, shops, library, and other services. Women and men were equal and independent, and sexual morality was not defined by legal norms. This was, at least, the blueprint.

Such solutions relied on individual self-transformation, and they were in principle rejected by the theoreticians of the socialist labor movement. Much as Marx and Engels were beguiled by Fourier's statement that "the degree of emancipation of women is the natural measure of general emancipation,"[4] they had no use for his phalanxes, as he called his communes, or for Cabet's "Icaria." The *Communist Manifesto* in 1848 dismissed the utopians and their colonies as "reactionary sects" lacking "all practical value and all theoretical justification . . . pocket editions of the New Jerusalem . . . castles in the air," requiring their founders "to appeal to the feelings and purses of the bourgeoisie."[5]

Nevertheless, Engels drew on the utopian socialist inheritance when he predicted, some 35 years later in discussing women's emancipation under socialism, that

> with the passage of the means of production to common property, the individual family ceases to be the economic unit of society. Private housekeeping is transformed into social industry. The care and education of children becomes a public matter. . . .[6]

When August Bebel, the founder of the German Social Democratic Party, attempted to fill in this picture in his *Woman under Socialism*, he assumed that the development of modern technology would make central kitchens and laundries for workers a matter of course.

In the first workers' state, however, experiments in communal living and dining were short-lived. They occurred in the period of famine and war communism immediately following the Bolshevik Revolution of 1917. The Soviet Union was unable to create the basic conditions for their success, and as a result they assumed the character of emergency housing and feeding arrangements which were abandoned when more conventional family life became possible. Alexandra Kollontai was one of a handful who saw collective housekeeping not just as a convenience for women but as part of the structure necessary for creating socialist relationships.[7]

Communes as a way of breaking out of the nuclear family,

overcoming the alienation of the individual, and liberating women arose in Sweden in the 1960s as they did in other Western countries. There are no estimates of how widespread the movement was or is, but it is apparent that communes in Sweden appeal to the same rather limited group as elsewhere: primarily young urban intellectuals. A young woman journalist in Stockholm described communal life in 1969 as offering more love, less fear, and less egoism. She wrote:

> The practical problems are legion. No one builds communal family flats
> . . . even though it would be economically profitable for society to invest in them. The communal family is simply not a common alternative yet. . . . This is where the mass media have a responsibility, which they of course have shirked. A constructive debate, information, and analysis could have made the communal family alternative of interest to city planners and architects, building firms, social scientists, and the ordinary man in the street.[8]

Communes do appear to suit certain people for at least certain periods of their life; some of these associations last a long time, others break up. Members are enthusiastic, ex-members complain that the commune exercises the same kind of constraints and emotional demands as the family. In its first manifesto at the end of the sixties, the Swedish feminist organization Group 8 called for the assignment of 25 percent of all new housing to collectives. Needless to say, this did not happen. Today, however, it seems feasible to combine some of the features of the commune and the collective house in various flexible arrangements which might make them appeal to a wider Swedish public as a reasonable alternative. The collective house differs from the commune in offering housekeeping services in common without attempting to regulate the lives of individual families.

Dick Urban Vestbro, an architect and assistant professor at the Royal Institute of Technology in Stockholm, has investigated the history of collective houses in Sweden, pointing out that two nineteenth-century Swedish authors, Carl Almquist and August Strindberg, were inspired by Fourier's ideas to write enthusiastically about the way relations between men and women could be improved by eliminating the nuclear family as the housekeeping unit.[9] The first interest by Swedish socialists in collective housing as a solution for workers occurred in the early 1930s, with Social Democratic women and Communists urging in vain a radical approach to workers' housing. A proposal for a collective housing unit by Alva Myrdal and Sven Markelius (later to become chief town planner for Stockholm) met with a hostile reception; such ideas were thought to stem from the Soviet Union and were regarded as threatening attempts to undermine the family.

In fact, according to Vestbro's review, it was the functionalist movement in Sweden which, in the spirit of Le Corbusier's "machine for living," predicted that the collective house would take its place alongside the rented flat and the private home to house the new type of family in which the woman was employed and the children were cared for in day nurseries. Several collective houses were built in Stockholm in the late 1930s and early 1940s, but most of them eventually foundered on the high service charges and the cost of operating a dining room without opening it to outsiders (and thus losing its unifying value for the collective).

In the postwar years building contractor Olle Engqvist built several collective housing units in Stockholm, two of which functioned successfully until 1976. The smaller one, built in 1944, with 200 flats providing one to three rooms and a kitchenette, was intended for working parents. The building included a laundry, shops, a day nursery for the residents' children, and a communal dining room. Tenants were required to subscribe to a minimum of 21 meals per month for ten months of the year so that the restaurant could maintain its family character. The meals were good but not inexpensive, and the flats were very modest in size. Nevertheless, in the 1970s the building still appealed to professionals who were willing to forfeit a larger and more modern flat, and perhaps a car or a weekend cottage, in favor of less housework and a friendly community. In 1976 the owner claimed he could no longer make ends meet, and the restaurant was closed down.

The Hässelby family hotel, built by the same contractor in the mid-1950s, was designed on a larger scale but tenants who wanted to use the restaurant still had to subscribe to a fixed number of meals. Three hundred and thirty apartments are grouped in four high-rise towers and 13 small blocks, all connected by enclosed corridors. The complex has a wide range of services including a youth center, a day-care center, a gym, medical services for the elderly, and a hobby workshop. The hotel, with apartments ranging from one to five rooms and a full-sized kitchen, attracted young people with radical and feminist views.

Tenants' representatives eventually came into conflict with the owner over the way the restaurant was run. When the owner got permission to close the restaurant in 1976, a group of tenants took over and ran it themselves, doing all the work on a rotation basis, serving dinners to several hundred people daily for a period of three years. In July 1979 the owner announced that he was going to use the dining-room premises for other purposes, and the tenants responded with a sit-in until they were carried out bodily by the police. Eleven of the tenants were taken to the police station and had charges preferred against them (later dropped). Among those arrested was feminist journalist Ami Lönnroth, a writer for the daily *Svenska Dagbladet*, who gave the event wide publicity and drew considerable public support. The tenants' group transferred its operations to the coffee lounge where it continued to serve simple meals, using donated kitchen equipment. Even though it then took two hours to wash dishes by hand, mothers and fathers of small children and single individuals still found the advantages worth the work involved. Pensioners who chose to join the group were exempt from kitchen detail. All the political parties except the Conservatives expressed support for the tenants.

The most recently built and largest collective house in Stockholm, known as Sollentuna, was completed in 1972 and is municipally owned. This mammoth complex with 1,250 flats and the full complement of schools, day-care centers, common rooms, a gym, doctors' offices, and shops differs from the service houses described earlier only in that it has a communal dining room. This, however, is also open to the public and tenants are not required to subscribe to a given number of meals. Critics have complained that the house is too big to foster a true communal spirit. Nevertheless, after some initial difficulties it became very popular and there are no empty apartments.

All these experiences with collective housing have stimulated a new debate, with slightly different terms of reference. Laundry and cleaning are now seen as tasks that can be done at home with relatively small effort—and for which personnel is not, in any case, available. The most important services demanded are the dining room and day care. The emphasis is on "solidarity, security, and spontaneous opportunities for contact." Collective housing holding out the possibility for more intimacy is being built by the municipality of Linköping, about 100 miles south of Stockholm. It will have 186 flats, of which 35 are designed for the elderly and nine for the handicapped. The tenants will be selected to represent a cross section of the population and will take part in study circles to prepare them for participation in planning and running the communal facilities.

Although in Stockholm there is said to be a long waiting list for collective housing, the Social Democratic and Liberal women's organizations favor it, and encouraging conditions have been extended to contractors for the installation of services, no one else is in a hurry to proceed to the planning stage. According to Vestbro, there are still too many doubts about how to combine the benefits of collective life with financial viability and how much direct tenant involvement would be productive. Karin Ahrland, Liberal MP and Chairperson of the Equality Committee, attributes the reluctance to the fact that although there are politicians in every party who favor collective housing, there are not enough of them on the Stockholm City Council: "Every man wants his Mom's meat balls." Vestbro himself endorses the conclusion of the Hässelby tenants that collective housing is incompatible with private ownership of the building, and that even municipalities must be led to see that a really collective house requires giving the tenants an active say; the tenants in turn must be prepared to accept responsibility. If the residents carry out part of the work themselves, as they are doing in Hässelby, it should be possible to cut costs enough so that collective housing need not be a middle-class privilege.

The Equality Committee stresses that it is not just housing but total planning—jobs, housing and transport—which must be changed to take account of equality between the sexes. Employment, including jobs for women, must be an essential part of all regional and local plans. In the words of a committee representative, Agneta Dreber:

> Housing must be built for cooperation. Perhaps you may even sometimes have to bring pressure on people to work together. Distances must be diminished between shops, work, services, day care. There should be small day-care centers right in the place where you live.

In the committee's view, people are interested in service houses but they do not care for large collective dining rooms and do not want to commit themselves to eating in them daily. It is time to try something else. One idea is to build for "extended families," adapting existing housing structures. This is where communes might find their needs fulfilled. Many of the earliest postwar residential areas need modernizing to bring them up to current standards. There are empty flats, for example, that could be combined and remodeled to meet the needs of a particular group. The university town of Göteborg has donated a block of flats dating from the 1950s for an architectural research project along these lines.

The Equality Committee has held a competition for architects who were asked to plan for the 1990s, and has published some of the best ideas as a set of panels that can be used as an exhibition by local groups. All of the suggestions break up the long rows of houses and the large apartment complexes and substitute small groups of houses or low blocks built around green space that can be used for common purposes. Space between existing blocks can be transformed into common gardens and playgrounds, assuming that the nineties will see fewer automobiles and more reliance on public transport. A group of small houses can acquire or build an additional structure with workshops and places for children and adults to meet indoors. Large housing estates can be built in subunits with their own services and facilities, all within reasonable distance of small, nonpolluting industries whose workshops are included in the overall plan. Designs for collective living include a two-family house with some common facilities; two apartments for couples, separated by a common living room and kitchen; adjoining apartments for a family with small children and a grandparent, with individual cooking facilities and living rooms that can be opened into each other. A similar arrangement would do for a couple with an adolescent child. A larger collective house for one large family, two small families and a single individual or couple, for example, could have a common children's playroom, dining room, and kitchen, and one or more TV rooms and sitting rooms. All these units are designed for privacy as well as sociability. One community, the municipality of Upplands-Väsby some 20 miles outside Stockholm, proposes to build eight collective houses of four households each, the degree of collectivity to be decided by the future tenants. Two hundred and fifty people expressed interest in the project at the drawing-board stage.

The way back from the depopulated city centers, the gigantic
cliff dwellings of the sixties, and the suburban spread of the seventies is very long, but there is nothing impractical about the best
service houses or the newest collective ideas. Business interests
raise objections to the idea of decentralizing industrial production
to the extent envisioned in the Equality Committee's concept of
total planning. Such decentralization is, however, one of the major
demands of the Center Party, to which Karin Andersson, the Minister for Equality, belongs. She believes it is no more impractical
to create jobs where people live than to transport the same people
45 minutes to their job and 45 minutes back every day. This is
probably the only practical way of creating diversified job opportunities for women. "Of course there are difficulties," she counters,
"but if we mean anything by equality we have to start somewhere."

Notes

1. Alexander Szalai, *The Use of Time* (The Hague: Mouton, 1972).
2. Gösta Carlestam and Lennart Levi, *Urban Conglomerates as Psycho-
social Human Stressors: A Contribution to the U.N. Conference on the Human
Environment* (Stockholm: Ministry of Foreign Affairs, 1972), p. 29.
3. Margaret Mead, "New Towns to Set New Life Styles," in Irving
Lewis Allen, ed., *New Towns and the Suburban Dream* (Washington: National
University Publishers, 1977) pp. 246-47.
4. The passage from Fourier containing this line is quoted with approval
in K. Marx and F. Engels, *The Holy Family*, (Moscow: Progress Publishers, 1975)
p. 230. Engels also refers to it in *Anti-Dühring* (New York: International Publishers, 1939), p. 284. Compare: "From this relationship (of man to woman)
one can . . . judge man's whole level of development," in Marx, *Economic and
Philosophical Manuscripts 1844* (Moscow: Foreign Languages Publishing
House, n. d.), p. 101.
5. K. Marx and F. Engels, "The Communist Manifesto" in *A Handbook
of Marxism* (New York: International Publishers, 1935), p. 57.
6. F. Engels, *The Origin of the Family, Private Property and the State*,
(Moscow: Foreign Languages Publishing House, 1948), p. 108.
7. A full discussion of Kollontai's views and her conflicts with the
Bolshevik Party over this and related issues appears in Cathy Porter's
Alexandra Kollontai: A Biography (London: Virago, 1980), esp. pp. 313-
43.
8. Quoted in B. Linnér, *Sex and Society in Sweden* (New York: Harper
Colophon, 1972), p. 129.
9. Dick Urban Vestbro, "Collective Housing Units in Sweden," *Current
Sweden* 234 (1979). This is the English text of Vestbro's "Kollektivhus i
Sverige 1900-1980," *BFL Rapport* 4:1979, which is illustrated. Much of the
information in the following paragraphs is taken from this monograph and
from a personal communication from Vestbro (April 25, 1980).

CHAPTER 9

Challenging the Imbalance of Power

Role sharing means power sharing, and there's the rub. Swedish women have the highest representation in parliament of any Western country, 25 percent of seats, having edged ahead of Norway with 24 percent and Denmark and Finland with 23 percent of the total. Women's growing political consciousness is a feature of all the political parties. The number of seats held by women in the Swedish parliament has risen from 50 in 1972 to 89 out of a total of 351 in the 1979 elections, compared to 19 out of 635 in the United Kingdom. Numerical advances have been made not only by Social Democratic women, who increased their places from 29 to 42, and by Communists, but by women in the parties to the right (See Table 10). Women have also strengthened their position on their parties' executives, especially in the Conservative and Liberal parties where they occupy well over one-third of the seats.

Swedes are a nation of joiners, dating back, it is said, to the popular religious, temperance, labor, and cooperative movements of the eighteenth and nineteenth centuries. They are considered to have "the most highly developed system of interest groups in the world," according to one Swedish political science professor, Nils Elvander of the University of Uppsala.[1] This helps to explain the strength and activity of the women's organizations attached to the political parties except for the Communist, which, true to communist tradition, has no separate women's organization. (The Communist Party does, however, have a Standing Committee on Feminism, and in 1979 the party strongly endorsed a feminist program which became one of its more important electoral issues.) The Social Democratic Party, with its long history as the policy-making party in Sweden, has attracted socially motivated women who, as has been seen, have insisted on a role in formulating that policy. Alva Myrdal is the best known of a long line of active women who have kept the organization from becoming a tea-giving backup club for a male party.

More revealing of the new trend toward an independent women's stance is the metamorphosis that has taken place in the women's organization of the Center Party. While the party polled only 18 percent of the vote at the 1979 elections, the Association of Swedish Center Women has 75,000 members compared to the Social Democratic Women's 50,000. This network grew out of the Center Party's original status as the farmers' party; its clubs provided social life and stimulus for rural women and its holiday homes offered them a much needed rest from drudgery. Although the party now has many manual workers and small businessmen among its members, its base is still in the rural areas, and its strength is its environmental and anti-nuclear policy. More than one-third of Center Party MPs are now women, and they are a driving force in the anti-nuclear power campaign. Since 1973 the women's organization has undertaken systematic education of its women in equality questions and has urged them to join trade unions. A special point of concentration has been the attitudes of children and the involvement of boys in domestic work. "But," says Christina Andersson, executive secretary of the organization,

> we have trouble with our men, although the younger ones are better than the older ones. But people in political life have arranged their own lives in a conservative way, and it is difficult to talk to them because we are challenging their private lives.

The Liberal Party women's organization keeps no central membership lists and tends toward the belief that separate women's organizations have outlived their usefulness. Liberal women see the future of women's political work in *ad hoc* groups cutting across party lines. Theirs is, however, the only political women's organization that has succeeded in introducing a quota system into party life. According to a 1972 party decision, women must have at least 40 percent representation on all party bodies, and they now hold 44 percent of posts on the executive committee.

There is considerable overlap among the three partisan women's organizations on specific issues, concerning which each is more militant than its respective party. All consider the six-hour day the most important single condition for progress on equality. The Liberals side with the Social Democrats in giving priority to day care over more supports for childcare in the home and in favoring legislation requiring fathers to share parental leave, while they agree with the Center Party women in backing a piecemeal reduction in the working day by automatically giving shorter hours to parents of small children.

This convergence is symptomatic of a growing impatience. Many "equality" issues were settled, in principle at least, under Social Democratic governments, and progress on most of them has continued since the center-right coalition came to power. Although no gains are necessarily irreversible, the rights to abortion, day care, parental leave, legal rights for persons living in "nontraditional" relationships, social-security protection for each person as an individual, and labor-market and educational measures directed at reducing sex-role stereotyping all appear to have a strong consensus behind them. Disagreement centers around timing, tactics, and details. The media take the equality debate seriously and generally give it substantial coverage.

These accomplishments have cleared the way for appraisal of how little such gains have actually affected the balance of power between men and women and the ability of women to affect the shape of the future. Women hold five out of 20 ministerial posts in government (1980), and about one-fourth of the seats, on average, in county and municipal governments (they account for as much as 45 percent of members in the Stockholm City Council). But in the 362 government committees with more than 5,500 members, women in 1978 held only 15 percent of the seats. These, moreover, were concentrated in education, social-service, and labor-market committees. Women averaged only 2 percent of places on economic and 8 percent of places on industrial committees. Among labor and employer representatives on county employment boards there are only five women, or 3.6 percent. There are no women among the 460 directors of associations in the Confederation of Swedish Employers.

In academia women are 3 percent of university professors, 7 percent of assistant professors and 13 percent of university lecturers. According to the Committee on Equality: "Because of failure to obtain research appointments, many questions are only studied from a male vantage point. This applies to education and social planning."[2]

Are those people right who say that sex-role equality is just a matter of time? Is it a noble but impractical dream, or are there concrete obstacles to its fulfillment that can be removed?

The Swedish sex-role equality program represented a qualitative advance because, unlike all previous government-sponsored movements to obtain equality for women, it did not propose simply to change women's status but recognized the need to change men's position as well. Those who formulated the goals did not then see a contradiction in changing the role of men within a constellation of circumstances that men themselves had created. They did not realize the extent to which men had a vested interest in that constellation, and that even men with liberal or radical views wanted nothing more than a redistribution of power and resources among men.

The Swedish model of new relations between women and men was strongly weighted with an economic determinism that has never been absent from socialist or Social Democratic practice anywhere, although it was modified by the characteristic Swedish concern for individual rights and the importance of self-realization. It was believed that judicious use of legislation, social policies, economic pressure, and education could change people's thinking and behavior patterns in a relatively short time. It was taken for granted that people absorb from their environment the messages that are left there for them by their leaders and the molders of public opinion, and that they do not distort them or screen them out.

The ideologists of equality thought that by giving boys and girls a solid biological knowledge of the facts of life and making contraceptives available they would take the doubts and irrationalities out of sexual life, and that by making the same education available to all and teaching girls metalwork and boys housekeeping the sexes would be reconditioned. The knowledge that great diversity had existed in the roles assigned to the sexes in various societies and at various periods in history, so that it was impossible to say that any combination of social tasks was inevitably male or female, led to the belief that it was possible to create a society in which virtually any task could be performed by either a woman or a man. But the difficulty of shifting from *some kind* of division of labor according to sex to a complete interchangeability of roles was not immediately apparent.

"Our debate on sex roles was very sophisticated," says

Birgitta Wistrand, president of the Fredrika Bremer Association. "It had to do with education and politics. It didn't go into people's minds or consciousness or their personal views. It wasn't necessary for *me* to change. This is still the official view on equality in Sweden. There has to be formal equality, and that's that."

Certainly in the early days of the sex-role equality debate the Social Democratic Party did not envision a power conflict between men and women, or a radical modification of party goals or of the shape of an ultimately socialist society—to be achieved by male working class power taking over the operation of the economy. There would simply be a kind of trade-off: men would contribute more in the home, women more in production. Olof Palme, Prime Minister and leader of the Swedish Democratic Party, told a women's audience in Washington, D.C. in 1970:

> The new role of the man implies that he must reduce his contributions in the working life—and maybe also in politics—during the period when he has small children. This is what the women always had to do alone earlier. From a national economy point of view we could manage this loss in production if we can instead stimulate the women to make increased contributions there.[3]

There was still a lot of irrational prejudice, to be sure, but this would gradually be eradicated by changing the social expectations on men and women. The burdens on the male—pressure to succeed, lack of contact with children, inability to express emotion, resulting in illness due to stress, higher criminality than women and a shorter life expectancy—were assumed to be burdens the male would gladly shed.

> The work toward equality between the sexes must be achieved jointly by men and women and not in struggle against each other. It should be carried out within the framework of strong political and trade union organizations because it necessitates changing society.[4]

At this point, in 1970, it was not yet clear that because these strong trade unions and political parties were male-dominated it would be men—presumably Social Democratic men—who would be establishing the ground rules governing work for equality. This gave to the early days of the campaign a deceptively bland and conflict-free character which appealed to observers who were put off by what they viewed as the noisy contentiousness of feminists in other countries. Linda Christmas, a member of the staff of the British *Guardian*, wrote at the end of 1975, International Women's Year:

> ... It is gratifying to find that Sweden has to a greater extent than other countries forsaken ideological rhetoric for practical reform and that, above all, it has made the sex-role argument respectable. This has been achieved because the Swedish Government, in ardent pursuit of its egalitarian principles, took the struggle for equality under its wing sufficiently early, thereby preventing the strident lobbyists turning the whole thing into a yawn.[5]

But the more legislative and social-policy problems were solved, or at least dealt with, in the framework provided by strong political and trade-union organizations, the more it was possible to see deeper conflicts underneath. It is an unplanned bonus of the Swedish equality drive that, with "practical reforms" largely agreed upon, it is possible to see the outlines of larger issues and speculate about the shape of things to come.

Although there were individual men like Palme himself in Sweden who were personally convinced of the need for a change in men's way of life, the missionary work in the early years was undertaken by women. In the very year Linda Christmas praised Sweden's harmonious debate, one of the originators of the "emancipation of man" concept, Karin Westman-Berg, told an interviewer:

> At first I thought the best way of getting anywhere would be for us to help men to discover the joy of coming closer to their children and having close relations with their families, of entering the private sphere which had formerly been reserved for us women.

> But now I can see that this will not be enough. Men in positions of political power who are favorably disposed towards an alteration of the traditional male roles still do not give priority to measures aimed in this direction. So the gains that men could derive from the new order of things are not as valuable to them as the advantages of the old system.

> ... We will have to go on and draw attention to the unconscious mechanisms in the role of the man and the construction of male society. ... The emancipation of man will have to overcome two obstacles. First

there is the way in which men themselves are oppressed through the
stultification of their emotional possibilities. (This is where we began in
the 1950s.) But then there is also the way in which men themselves
function as oppressors . . .[6]

In a society as aflluent and pervasively benevolent as Sweden,
it is difficult to pinpoint the causes of dissatisfaction and easy to
be lulled into believing that everything is being taken care of by
someone else. Berit Rollén, a director of the Labor Market Board
who is personally strongly committed to work for equality, has
commented more than once, "We here at the Labor Market Board
are the militant ones. We can't find any signs of women who are
dissatisfied. They do the housework and accept part-time jobs.
Why are we forcing them?" She would like to see women out in
the streets demanding men's jobs as they earlier demanded more
day care. But then she offers her own explanation for what she
sees as apathy: "The questions have become very subtle. How do
you fight satisfaction? How do you fight politicians who say, we
are with you all the way?"

Liljeström's investigations in Kristianstad County (see Chapter 2) showed her how women's awareness of their special potential had developed out of the resistance they had experienced
when they sought more independence, but she did not find this
paralleled by women's consciousness of their collective strength.
She noted, in her report to the government's Committee on Equality:

> Women, if they are to achieve their collective liberation, need to rally
> around a community of values, around a program which roots them in
> shared experiences and which gives them political identity for "sister-
> hood" and an alternative value system to keep them from being de-
> voured by an equality under the terms set by the male value system.
> For women's liberation is about something more than "to pass off as a
> man." It is about changing destructive features in a man's society.[7]

It is a paradox of the Swedish welfare state that it has absorbed so many feminist demands, and yet women in Sweden appear to find it even more difficult than they do elsewhere to keep
"from being devoured by equality under the terms of a male value
system." There is a certain logic in it, however. Men feel that they
have "done a great deal for women" and are probably going to do
a great deal more, but they expect it all to be done in the frame-

work of existing male institutions. General precepts about men's right to be more loving are fine, but challenges that go to the very essence of male-ordered society—that's hitting below the belt. Many women who are disappointed because things are going so slowly are still reluctant to risk a "backlash" from men who have shown themselves so "reasonable." There is probably no Western country where hostility to "feminism" as opposed to "women's liberation" is so out of proportion to the strength and militancy of the avowed feminists in the women's movement.

"Feminist" is used here to define those who see women as oppressed and men as oppressors and believe that the radical reordering of society, which they consider necessary for the elimination of sex roles, requires the recognition of this major conflict and its resolution. These are the women who, beginning with consciousness-raising groups—in which they have tried to develop the ideology and "identity for sisterhood" of which Liljeström writes—have branched out into concrete attempts to construct an alternative value system. At the grassroots level one finds feminist theatres, publishers, bookstores, cafés, refuges for battered women, rape victim centers, self-help medical groups. At the academic level feminism has initiated research that questions the inevitability of male institutions and the male angle of vision. Such initiatives are flourishing in Denmark, Great Britain, and the United States; they are rare, however, in Sweden.

The only clearly identifiable feminist network, considered to be the most radical constellation of Swedish women, is Group 8. It has, in fact, only recently begun to identify itself as feminist. According to Ebba, one of the editors of their bi-monthly *Kvinnor bulletinen*:

> At the beginning we identified ourselves as women socialists. We were very afraid of the word feminist—we too! We organized in a very traditional left way, except that we were women. We put socialism ahead of feminism, and we were constantly asking ourselves what the men on the left would think of us.

Group 8 is still organized along conventional lines compared to the feminist movements in other countries which emphasize lack of hierarchy and informality as the antithesis of male power structures. It has elaborate statutes, regular meetings, dues, and congresses. Its clubs are only now beginning to use consciousness-raising as a method of work, explicitly following the model of Denmark and Great Britain. According to its own estimates, Group 8 had in 1979 only 90 dues-paying members in Stockholm and a few thousand in the country as a whole, although its following is undoubtedly much greater than these figures indicate, since its magazine, sold only on street corners and in alternative bookstores, has a circulation of about 9,000. Group 8's program, which has not changed in the past decade, differs little from what many "establishment" women are asking: work for every woman; the six-hour day for everyone; free day care for all; protection of a woman's right to her own body; better contraception; protection of the right to abortion on demand; collective houses and service houses.

So it is not the size of the organization or its demands that make Group 8 a kind of bogey, but the fact that they preach confrontation rather than conciliation. Women who press for action too frequently and too sharply at equality-committee meetings on the job are reprimanded with, "Oh, you're one of those Group 8 women!" "If I'd known you were a member of Group 8 I'd never have hired you," one of the editors of the Group 8 magazine was told by the headmaster of the school where she teaches. To Group 8 women in turn it is incredible that the Advisory Council on Equality celebrated International Women's Year in 1975 with a big exhibition on men (see Chapter 3). Gunilla says:

> The official view in Sweden is that men are as oppressed as women. We don't think it's our job to change men's opinions. If men have realized they are so terribly oppressed, it's up to them to do something about it. First they tell you how badly off the women are in other countries, then how badly off men are, and then they want to know how you can ask for more favors, although you are actually demanding your rights.

Group 8 women acknowledge that a major obstacle to feminist militancy is the fact that the sex-role equality program in Sweden has won concrete gains which feminists in other countries have so far not achieved. It sees as its main role the development of a different way of living, the definition of that "community of values" which Liljeström advocated in her report. Here it feels itself up against a characteristic aspect of Swedish life that is raised by every advocate of spontaneous public participation, whether it is more involvement of parents in day care or of tenants in improving their neighborhood or of trade unionists in teaching children: "there is no space for us to experiment." The territory is occupied. There is already an organization or an agency taking care of the problem. There is an orderly, reasonable Swedish way of bringing about change, which does not include grassroots alternatives.

That there is still need for individual initiative from the bottom was dramatically demonstrated nonetheless, when the extent of physical violence against women by men was exposed. This was not the work of a government investigating commission. It was brought to light by two women journalists, Karin Alfredsson and Ulla Lemberg. In a book published at the end of 1979, *A Man Beats the One He Loves*, they disclosed that 300,000 Swedish women are known to be mishandled by men each year, and that in 40–60 cases the injuries are fatal. Women are rarely willing to prefer charges against their assailants; of 500 women admitted to the emergency department of one Stockholm hospital with signs of violence all over their bodies, only 40 admitted that they had been beaten by their husband. According to the authors, the violence against women is not restricted to "problem families" or to men who have been drinking or those who have missed the civilizing influence of higher education. In the parliamentary debate which resulted from this exposé, the Minister of Justice (the only male who took the floor) declared that society had pretended for too long that nothing was going on, and stated that the law would be changed to enable a third party to bring charges in such cases so that the conspiracy of silence could be broken.[8]

The new spirit in the Fredrika Bremer Association may be taken as a gauge of the shift toward the more emphatic expression of women's consciousness and a clearer definition of the areas in which men's and women's interests clash. A politically unaffiliated organization nearly 100 years old, carrying the name of Sweden's foremost nineteenth-century fighter for women's rights, its appeal is primarily to educated middle-class women. Among its 8,000 members it also numbers about 300 men who feel strongly about women's rights. Although it has taken a firm stand on sex-role equality questions, its traditional image was that of a polite debating society which tried to spread the word without offending anyone. According to Birgitta Wistrand, who has been the association's president since 1976:

Women haven't asked for the formal power and they haven't asked for the informal power. One of the difficult things in Sweden is that women have been brought up to be very polite and it's hard for them to get on their feet in a debate and say I stand for this and that. Women who are strong personalities don't get elected.

Since Wistrand took office the association has changed both its outer and its inner work. It goes out into the streets campaigning for more women in public office, and at the same time it has turned its attention to changing individual attitudes. It is now also working with consciousness-raising (women and men in separate groups and some mixed groups) on the Danish model, in which a new consciousness has to be followed by action:

> It's important that women take leadership, that they learn how to handle power, to handle conflicts. It's important to be aggressive, but in a very matter of fact way, to go in and say, "This is what we want and you have to do something and we won't stop until you do."

Swedish men don't expect this. When Wistrand criticized the government publicly in 1978 because there were only six women out of twenty ministers, two male ministers called her to tell her she was too negative and she shouldn't say things like that. When she walked into the stockholders' meeting of a company in which the association is a shareholder and said there should be some women on the board, "they were so startled that there was chaos for 15 minutes until they could settle the parliamentary procedure for handling such an issue!"

Wistrand, in common with some other Scandinavian observers of the political scene, believes that now that women are in politics, "the power has moved to the trade unions where there are few women, and to the employers where there are no women."

> Here in Sweden you don't admit that you have the power. It's the members' power! But if you go and look, the power is at the very top, and the top works together with the political bosses and they work together with the top employers, and on equality the employers and the labor unions have the same point of view; they are working for the same goal.

The unions don't expect to hear this either, and the few women who have risen in the ranks have, in Wistrand's opinion, absorbed the outlook of a male society. She protested to the Metalworkers'

Union, the largest union in Sweden with 75,000 women among its 460,000 members, when they held a congress with 300 delegates of whom three were women.

> They were going to discuss their equality program. I asked them, "How can you do this? Is this a real step to equality?" What happened? The three women appeared with me on TV and said that they were quite satisfied. They thought the men could take care of equality as well as they!

In a running debate in the press, the Confederation of Trade Unions has charged the Fredrika Bremer Association with being too aggressive and working for the wrong type of woman. LO is not used to having "outsiders interfere with its problems."

A confrontation of value systems is the inevitable consequence of an issue which has far greater implications for the future of society than any mentioned so far—atomic power. This has been a women's issue in Sweden since 1972 when a woman MP, Birgitta Hambraeus of the Center Party, first raised in parliament the question of the disposal of nuclear waste and then called for a moratorium on the construction of new nuclear reactors. Although her motion failed, nuclear power—which until then had been taken for granted in Sweden—became the subject of fierce debate. In 1976 an anti-nuclear campaign mounted by the Center Party with the support of the Communist Party played a key role in bringing down the Social Democratic government. In the following years nuclear power became a focal point for women's activity. Women who had seemed apathetic about job issues were articulate when it came to atomic power. Kvinnokamp för fred (Women's Struggle for Peace) a non-party *ad hoc* group, linked the fight against nuclear power to the struggle against the proliferation of nuclear weapons and organized a number of successful mass demonstrations and marches. Among women who in recent years have devoted practically all of their energy to informing the public of the hazards of nuclear power is the journalist Eva Moberg, who is credited with launching the sex-role equality debate in the early sixties.

Nuclear power has been difficult to oppose in Sweden, since 75 percent of the country's energy needs are covered by imported oil and there are no known sources of natural gas. In the event of the total rejection of nuclear power as the alternative to oil, Sweden would be heavily dependent on the development of new types of energy—solar, wind, and geothermal. It is thus impossible to conceive of a nuclear-powerless Sweden without a revolution in life style based on zero growth or a reduction in growth. In spite of this, according to a poll conducted for the power industry in 1974, at the height of the oil crisis, 81 percent of the sample faored reduction of energy consumption even at the cost of their standard of living, and 59 percent expressed support for a delay in the development of nuclear power.

Nevertheless, Sweden continued to sail along, as it has for decades, on a philosophy of growth and ever-increasing consumption, backed both by industry as represented by the Conservative Party, and by organized labor under the banner of the Social Democrats. The expansion of the public sector, on which the welfare state depends, requires higher corporate profits and higher individual incomes on which taxes can be collected. It was only after the U.S. reactor accident at Three Mile Island in the spring of 1979 that the Social Democratic Party decided that the time had come to submit its pro-nuclear policy to public review and agreed to a referendum on the future of nuclear power.

There followed a confusing three-way referendum in 1980 in which voters were asked to decide whether they wanted the existing six nuclear power plants to be dismantled within ten years (as proposed by the Center and Communist parties), or would agree to the fueling of a further six newly built plants (as the other parties recommended) with the use of nuclear power to end with the natural life of the 12 plants, i.e., in 25–30 years. The only difference between the Conservatives on the one hand and the Social Democrats and Liberals on the other was that the latter two wanted complete state control over nuclear power.

The results were accepted abroad as a victory for nuclear energy, since 58 percent of the voters backed the 12-reactor proposal. In fact, however, both proposals involved the eventual dismantling of nuclear energy. In other words, the public was not even asked to vote on the policies advocated by industrialist and employer groups, who clearly favored unlimited nuclear expansion and invested heavily in pro-nuclear advertising.[9]

The fact that women closely identified with the sex-role equality debate were also associated with the anti-nuclear movement indicates the extent to which women now link equality not only with peace and disarmament but with a new life-style, different from the one envisioned by the strong political organizations and strong trade unions that were the original champions of their cause. The link is personified by Karin Andersson, whose career in the anti-nuclear Center Party has taken her from chairperson of the Stockholm Center Party's women's organization to chairperson of the government Committee on Equality, and finally to the post of Minister for Equality Affairs. Karin Söder, also of the Center Party, former Swedish Minister of Foreign Affairs, and Minister of Health and Social Affairs at the time of the referendum, served as a member of the "Anti-Nuclear Power" campaign board. Among those who broke with their party's position to work against nuclear power was the veteran diplomat Inga Thorsson, one of the Social Democratic Party's experts on disarmament and a Swedish advisor on disarmament and development at the United Nations.[10] It was she who back in the early sixties had chaired the party's "study group on women's questions" (Chapter 2) whose "Erlander Report" created the basis for the first legislative and policy changes directed at sex-role equality. Ulla Lindström, a former Social Democratic cabinet minister who also served as a member of the study group, is spending her retirement years working in the anti-nuclear energy movement.

Some months before the nuclear power referendum, Gunnar Qvist, the labor historian, commented:

> From the point of view of equality between the sexes the referendum will decide the future. If we choose atomic power it will be a society of male technocrats. Then we will need an army to protect the plants. Rejection of atomic energy will mean small-scale production involving wind and water.

No such clear-cut choice emerged from the referendum, but the technocratic society is still not inevitable. Debate over what the future will look like has been going on in Sweden for some time, and particularly since the U.N. conference on the human environment held in Stockholm in 1972. Generalized objections to the manipulation of the individual by technology, and dissatisfaction with institutionalized and professionalized methods of dealing with people's needs have been expressed in the context of shrinking resources, a deteriorating environment, and pressure for global solidarity. Swedish futurologists have proposed concrete first steps toward a different rather than a higher standard of living: a ceiling on energy consumption, a ceiling on meat consumption, more economical use of building space, controlled use of private automobiles, and consumer goods made to last, coupled with depressurized advertising.[11] The insistence on decentralization of government, more voice for workers in decision making, and government promises of support for small enterprises point to the desire for a return to a life of manageable dimensions.

So far these criticisms, analyses, and blueprints have been largely the work of men, and have not examined the way such changes would affect women's position specifically. The women's movement, in turn, although it has submitted a long list of needs and musts to parliament through the Committee on Equality,[12] has not produced its model of what a society based on sex-role equality would look like. Nevertheless, the Swedish experience of more than a decade in attempting to change society's expectations of women and men and bring them closer together does provide the basis for some general conclusions about what conditions appear to favor this effort and which do not.

It appears that a low-key, decentralized society, with emphasis on the participation of the individual in the life of the community and respect for the environment, and on shared work rather than more specialized commercial services, would be one in which equality could thrive. The women's movement envisions smaller-scale dwelling units, collective services, a closer relationship with children, and an end to the sharp distinction between the living and working environments. With job opportunities closer to home and a shorter working day providing more free time for family and neighborhood concerns, there would also be more likelihood of equality on the labor market.

Measures in support of this style of life have made little headway because they run counter to the needs of Sweden's predominantly privately owned production system for profitability and competitiveness. These needs, as has been seen, impede changes in working time, discourage a redivision of tasks in the home, and have something to do with perpetuating traditional choices by young people in education and the job world. This is not specific to Sweden but a recognized dilemma of the Western industrialized nations: while they need women available to the labor force and profess support for equality, they "cannot afford" concrete equality measures. At a meeting of labor ministers of the 24 countries belonging to the Organization for Economic Cooperation and Development, called to discuss working women in April 1980, OECD General-Secretary Emile van Lennep reportedly warned the member states that government measures to give women jobs might prove costly for management and "make their employment more difficult," that maternity leave, social-security provisions, "and in some instances equal pay" might increase production costs and ultimately harm women seeking jobs.[13] On the other hand, the alternative Social Democratic trade-union model of socialism, in which power over the economy is transferred to representatives of the male working class, does not appear to hold out better prospects for upgrading women's work, sharing power, or a more equal division of family responsibilities.

The alluring area of alternative life styles does have its potential dangers. It is easy to imagine that reduced dependence on a state-supported public sector, with the appealing prospect of making members of the community more responsible for each other and rehabilitating voluntary work, could strengthen traditional roles unless accompanied by strong counter-measures to ensure that such work was equally shared by men and women. It will by no means happen automatically in a minus-growth society or a society where production is directed at needs rather than profits that the social recognition given to unpaid work or work in the services will be adjusted to their social importance. Nor will the mechanism that tends to reproduce power in the hands of those who already have it wind down of itself.

It would be unrealistic to suppose that all Swedish women or all women anywhere can agree on exactly what the good society of the future should look like or exactly what steps are necessary to get there. What is likely to happen first is that they will insist that sex-role equality be made a priority question, an integral part of all plans for the future, and a criterion of the effectiveness of all policies and individual measures. It was assumed in the past that efforts to achieve greater equality among men would result in equality for women as a side effect, but this did not happen. Sex-role equality was discretely smuggled into the Swedish Equality Program in the sixties, somewhat the way women's rights were smuggled into Title VII of the Civil Rights Act in the United States.[14] But the Swedish experience is evidence that equality between women and men is not just another aspect of equality, on a par with equality for the races and nationalities, for the poor, the elderly, the handicapped, the rural population; it cuts across all these categories. Equality efforts that do not give priority to measures that promote equality between men and women can correct some gross injustices and achieve for women the formal guarantees that men already take for granted. But the gap between men and women at all levels—measured in terms of a voice in decision making, access to employment, earnings, life options, or leisure time—remains and is increasing. This is certainly true if account is taken of the fact that the powers men possess over resources, economies, life and death—powers women do not share—now have global rather than local consequences. Equality for all underprivileged groups, of which women make up in most cases at least 50 percent, can be achieved only together with equality for women. The radical nature of the upheaval involved has been remarked by Gunhild Kyle, who believes that "It will change men's lives totally. A feminist revolution will have to alter much more than the Industrial Revolution ever did."

Men have been slow to recognize the implications of the movement for equality. Thus, what can be expected in Sweden is continued but gradual progress along the path we have traced— from women's readiness to work for sex-role equality on men's terms, to an insistence that women have their own priorities, that men must cease doing women "favors" and change themselves, and that confrontation on matters of principle can take place between men and women just as it can between men and men, without losing sight of the ultimate goal of unity. And, given Sweden's record of designing policies and measures to meet new social situations, there is every reason to believe that Swedish women will be pioneers in the next phase of the women's liberation struggle— the development of a blueprint for a nonsexist society.

Notes

1. Nils Elvander, "Interest Groups in Sweden; Their Political Role,"

168   Sweden's "Right to be Human"

Current Sweden 48 (1974): 1.

2. "Report from the Swedish Government to the ECE seminar on the participation of women in the economic evolution of the ECE region" (Stockholm, March 1979), p. 23.

3. Olof Palme, "The Emancipation of Man," Address to the Women's National Democratic Club, Washington, D.C., June 8, 1970, Royal Swedish Embassy, Washington, D.C. (press release), pp. 8-9.

4. Ibid., p. 15.

5. Linda Christmas, "A Sexy Question," *Sweden Now* 3(1975): 25.

6. "The Emancipation of Men: Karin Westman-Berg interviewed by Ying Toijer-Nilsson," *Herta* 2 (1975): 7-8.

7. Rita Liljeström, Gunilla Fürst Mellström, and Gillan Liljeström Svensson, *Roles in Transition* (Stockholm: Liber Förlag, 1978), p. 177.

8. "Zu viele Schweden verprügeln ihre Frauen," *Die Presse* (Vienna), January 17, 1980.

9. The following issues of *Current Sweden* are devoted to the nuclear power debate: 51 (1974); 156 (1977); 177 (1977); 223 (1979); 245 (1980); 246 (1980).

10. Torsten Kälvemark, "Swedish Public Discussion on Nuclear Power," *Current Sweden* 245 (1980): 11.

11. Göran Bäckstrand and Lars Ingelstam, "We Could Remodel Sweden," *Current Sweden* 86 (1975).

12. The National Plan of Action for Equality presented to the Swedish government by the Committee on Equality between Men and Women is available in English as *Step by Step* (Stockholm: Liber Förlag, 1979).

13. "OECD Discusses Women in Labor Force," *International Herald Tribune*, April 17, 1980. The Eastern European socialist countries also "cannot afford" equality for somewhat different reasons. See Hilda Scott, *Does Socialism Liberate Women?* (Boston: Beacon Press, 1974).

14. See Introduction, note 5.

Appendix:
Tables and Figure

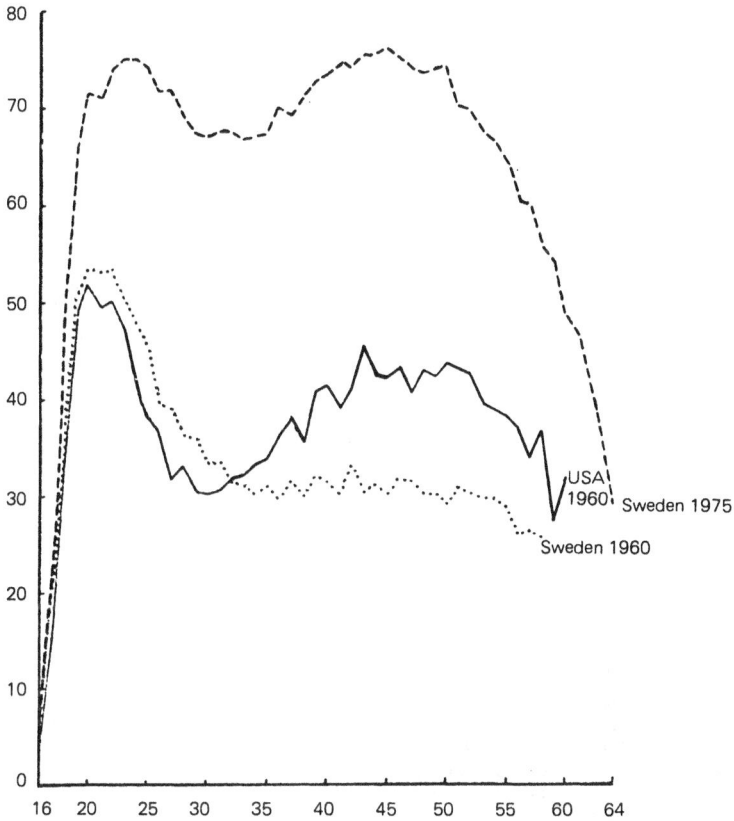

Figure 1. Female labor force participation rates. Cross sections 1960 for
Sweden and the United States, and 1975 for Sweden.

Source: Siv Gustafsson, Lifetime Patterns of Labor Force Participation (Paper presented
at the meeting of Scandinavian economists in Helsingør, Denmark, June 1979).

Table 1   **Social-Security Spending in Relation to GNP**
                 in Selected European Countries, 1966-1970

Country	Per capita GNP in U.S. dollars (1966)	Percent GNP spent on S.S. (1966)	Percent GNP spent on S.S. (1970)	Percent population over 60 (1970)
Austria	1225	21.0	23.4	20.1
Germany (FRG)	1871	19.6	22.6	19.4
Belgium	1690	18.5	19.5	18.9
Netherlands	1497	18.3	23.0	14.5
France	1866	18.3	20.9	18.0
Sweden	2677	17.5	22.1	19.6
Italy	1097	17.5	21.1	15.7
Czechoslovakia	1334	17.2	18.0	17.0
Germany (GDR)	1227	16.4	18.1	22.1
U.K.	1532	14.4	19.6	18.7
Hungary	895	11.0	11.1	17.1
Poland	762	9.4	10.9	12.8
USSR	1181	11.2	11.3	11.9

Source: Adapted from Kurt Bayer, "Economic Conditions and Social Services in Europe, 1970-1975," *Eurosocial Occasional Papers* No. 2 (Vienna: European Centre for Social Welfare Training and Research, 1976), p. 15.

Note: Social-security programs normally cover medical care, family allowances, maternity benefits, sickness benefits, death grants, employment injury, unemployment insurance, old-age, disability, and survivors' benefits.

Table 2   **Infant Mortality* in International Comparison, 1970**

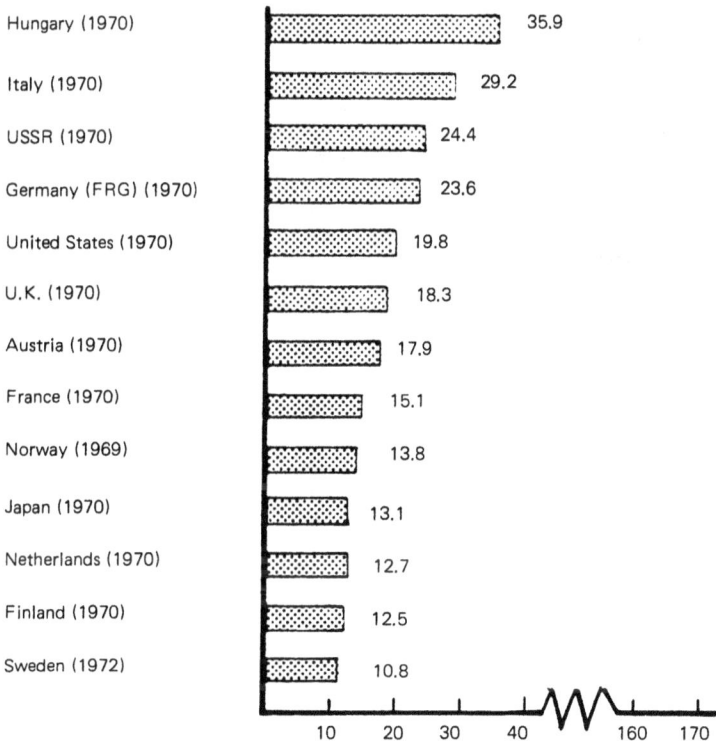

Country	Rate
Hungary (1970)	35.9
Italy (1970)	29.2
USSR (1970)	24.4
Germany (FRG) (1970)	23.6
United States (1970)	19.8
U.K. (1970)	18.3
Austria (1970)	17.9
France (1970)	15.1
Norway (1969)	13.8
Japan (1970)	13.1
Netherlands (1970)	12.7
Finland (1970)	12.5
Sweden (1972)	10.8

(axis: 10 20 30 40 160 170)

Source: P. Owe Petersson, "Child Health Services in Sweden," *Current Sweden*, No. 124 (June 1976).
*Deaths per 1,000 live births.

Table 3   Labor-Force Participation Rates of Women and Men Aged 15 to 64,
in Member Countries of the OECD (1975)

Country	Women	Men
Australia	49	89
Austria	48	84
Belgium	44	84
Canada	50	86
Denmark	64	90
Finland	66	80
France	57	84
Germany (FRG)	49	86
Greece	31	83
Ireland	45	94
Iceland	34	92
Italy	31	81
Japan	52	90
Luxembourg	31	86
Netherlands	27	84
New Zealand	39	88
Norway	53	86
Portugal	32	94
Spain	33	88
Sweden	68	89
Switzerland	55	95
Turkey	53	93
Great Britain	55	92
United States	53	85
Yugoslavia	46	85
Average	46	88

Source: *Siffror om Män och Kvinnor* [Men and Women: Key Figures], (Stockholm:
SAF, 1979), p. 288.

Table 4

Employed Persons by Sex and Industrial Branch in Sweden, 1963 and 1977

	1963			1977		
Industry	Men, percentage distribution	Women, percentage distribution	Women (%)	Men, percentage distribution	Women, percentage distribution	Women (%)
Agriculture, hunting, forestry, and fishing	15.3	8.7	24.9	7.8	3.7	26.3
Mining, manufacturing;	38.2	22.4	25.4	35.6	15.8	25.5
thereof, engineering industries	11.6	3.8	16.1	16.6	5.2	19.5
Construction	12.7	1.4	6.0	11.9	1.2	6.9
Trade, restaurants, and hotels;	11.8	22.9	52.9	12.2	17.4	52.4
thereof, trade	10.9	18.5	49.5	11.2	14.9	50.5
Transport, communication	9.1	4.3	21.6	8.8	4.2	27.0
Finance, insurance, etc.	3.1	5.5	50.7	5.6	6.4	46.5
Community, social and personal services;	9.7	34.6	67.5	17.7	51.4	69.1
thereof, public administration, education, health and welfare	8.2	25.7	64.5	12.5	45.4	73.7

Source: Swedish Labor Market Board, *The Swedish Labor Force Survey*, yearly averages for 1963 and 1977.

Table 5

**Distribution of the Female Work Force by Economic Sector
in Sweden and the Countries of the Common Market, 1975 (in %)**

	Agriculture	Industry	Services
Germany	8.8	30.9	60.3
France	8.8	25.1	66.2
Italy	14.5	33.9	51.7
Netherlands	1.7	17.2	81.1
Belgium	3.8	26.8	69.3
Luxembourg	8.7	13.7	77.6
United Kingdom	1.1	27.3	71.6
Ireland	7.8	25.7	66.5
Denmark	4.0	17.5	78.5
Europe of the Nine	7.1	28.1	64.8
Sweden (1977)	3.7	17.0	79.3

Sources: Statistical Office of the European Communities (Luxembourg), *Labor Force Sample Survey*, 1975; Swedish Labor Market Board, *The Swedish Labor Force Survey*, 1977.

Table 6

**Percentage of Women in Swedish Blue-Collar Trade Unions
(LO) and Trade-Union Offices, 1976**

Union	Women members	Congress delegates	National executive	Central negotiating board	Regional executives
Garment workers	68.2	45.0	29.0	20.0	33.0
Sheet metal workers	none	none	none	none	none
Building workers	1.7	0.81	none	none	5.25
Electricians	0.2	none	none	none	none
Factory workers	29.0	9.5	9.0	10.0	11.0
Maintenance workers	57.0	16.6	9.5	17.0	24.0
Hairdressers	90.1	58.6	29.0	40.0	65.0
Social-insurance and insurance agents	68.9	37.0	20.0	27.0	39.0
Graphic industry	25.1	5.0	5.8	5.8	13.0
Miners	8.1	3.0	none	none	n.a.
Retail and commercial employees	70.7	51.0	11.0	47.0	46.0
Hotel and restaurant	79.9	39.0	33.0	none	69.0
Municipal workers	76.8	33.5	45.0	45.0	33.0
Agricultural workers	17.4	1.75	none	7,6	5.0
Food	39.5	14.0	9.0	9.7	8.0
Metal workers	16.2	1.0	none	none	4.0
Musicians	17.2	n.a.	n.a.	n.a.	n.a.
Painters	0.1	none	none	none	none
Pulp and paper	16.9	4.0	none	none	7.0
Seamen	19.1	5.3	none	none	n.a.
Forest workers	4.8	4.0	none	none	1.6
Chimney sweepers	none	none	none	none	none
State employees	24.8	10.0	6.6	13.0	10.6
Transport workers	11.5	6.8	11.0	13.0	12.5
Wood industry	12.7	1.6	none	2.0	1.4
Total	35.6	15.0	9.0	14.0	13.0

Source: Calculated by the author from data in *Kvinnor i facket* [Women in Trade Unions] (Stockholm: LO, 1977).

Table 7

**Provision of Preschool Education in Western European Countries,
in Percent of Age Group Attending**

Country	Types of provision	Years	Age 2 (%)	Age 3 (%)	Age 4 (%)	Age 5 (%)	Age 6 (%)
Austria	NS	1975-76	—	- - - - - -44 - - - - - -			school
Belgium	NS			90	97	99	school
Cyprus	NS[a]	1976-77	—	15	25	school	
Denmark	DNS, PSC	1975-76	—	27	37	36	85
Germany (FRG)	NS, PSC	1975-76	—	- - - - - -70 - - - - - -			school
Finland	DNS	1975-76	—	- - - - - -15 - - - - - -			34
France	NS, NC	1975-76	26	79	97	99	school
Greece			not available				school
Iceland	NS, PSC	1977-78	21[b]	30[b]	23[b]	23[b]	91[b]
Ireland	PSC	1975-76	—	1	62	98	school
Italy	NS	1975-76	—	- - - - - -64 - - - - - -			school
Liechtenstein	NS	1976-77	—	—	—	98	98
Luxembourg	NS	1977-78	—	—	76	98	school
Malta	NS[a]	1975-76	—	—	81	school	
Netherlands	NS	1975-76	—	2	94	97	school
Norway	DNS, FDC	1975-76	5	8	11	13	16
Portugal	NS[a]	1975-76	—	- - - - - -12[b] - - - - - -			school
Spain	NS[a]	1974-75	—	—	50	76	school
Sweden	DNS	1977-78	10	13	17	33	98
Switzerland	NS	1976-77	—	4	16	53	68
Turkey			not available				
U.K.	NS, NC, PSC	1975-76	—	12	49	school	

Source: Martin Woodhead, "Pre-School Provision in Western Europe" (Paper presented at the conference "From Birth to Eight: Young Children in European Society in the 1980s," Council for Europe, Strasbourg, December 17-20, 1979), p. 10.

[a]Includes private nursery schools not receiving state funds.

[b]Stated to be estimate.

NS—Nursery schools   PSC—Primary school classes
NC—Nursery classes   FDC—Family day care
DNS—Day nursery schools

Table 8

Girls as Percent of Enrollment in the Swedish Integrated Upper Secondary School, by Study Line, 1971-1978

	1971	1973	1975	1977	1978
Two-Year Lines					
Clothing manufacturing	87	96	99	97	97
Consumer studies	97	98	97	98	98
Workshop	0	1	2	3	1
Electro-technical	0	1	2	2	2
Nursing	98	97	97	96	95
Technical	2	3	3	2	2
Three-Year Lines					
Liberal arts	80	80	81	83	84
Economics	46	50	53	51	53
Natural sciences	41	39	42	43	44
Social sciences	70	69	68	70	70
Four-Year Technical Line	7	5	8	12	11

Source: Swedish National Board of Education.

Table 9

Women as Percent of Enrollment in Selected Branches of University Study in Sweden, 1973 and 1978

	1973	1978
Library College	75	65
School of Pharmacy	59	69
Liberal Arts	63	66
Social Work & Public Administration	61	69
Social Science	36	44
Law	32	43
Mathematics & Natural Sciences	29	31
Theology	28	37
Technology	12	14
Medicine	29	35 (1976)

Source: Swedish National Board of Education.

Table 10

**Women as Members of the Swedish Parliament,
by Party, 1972, 1976, 1979**

Party	1972		1976		1979	
	Number	Percent	Number	Percent	Number	Percent
Conservative	4	10	7	13	16	21.9
Center	9	13	23	27	20	31.3
Liberal	5	9	8	21	9	23.7
Social Democratic	29	18	33	22	41	27.3
Communist	3	18	4	24	5	25.0
Total	50	14	75	21.5	91	25.9

Sources: *Women in Sweden in the Light of Statistics* (Stockholm: The Joint Female Labor Council, 1973), p. 94; *Siffror om Män och Kvinnor* (Stockholm: SAF, 1979),
p. 272; *Current Sweden*, No. 238 (1979); No. 248 (1980).

Index of Names

Index of Subjects

About the Author

Hilda Scott, a journalist who has spent much of her career abroad writing on European affairs, is the author of *Does Socialism Liberate Women? Experiences from Eastern Europe*, 1974 (British title *Women and Socialism*, 1976) and editor (with Margrit Eichler) of *Women and Futures Research*, 1981. Her articles on women's position in society have appeared in journals in the United States and Europe. She is also a member of the editorial advisory board of the British journal *Women's Studies International Quarterly*. She now makes her home in Cambridge, Massachusetts.

For Product Safety Concerns and Information please contact our EU
representative GPSR@taylorandfrancis.com
Taylor & Francis Verlag GmbH, Kaufingerstraße 24, 80331 München, Germany

9 781138 037939